Buttons, Bolt Cutters & Barricades

TEXAS ANTI-NUKE ACTIONS

Jerry Palmer

Copyright © 2021 by Jerry Palmer
All rights reserved. No part of this book may be used or reproduced in any manner whatsoever without written permission, except in the case of brief quotations embodied in critical articles and reviews.

Printed in the United States of America

ISBN 978-1-938819-90-2
Hardback 978-1-938819-91-9
ebook 978-1-938819-92-6

First Printing 2021

Written by Jerry Palmer, cover design by Shawn Palmer, edited by Susan Marquez

All images appearing in this book are courtesy of the Palmer Family Archives, The Dallas Morning News, Fort Worth Star - Telegram Collection, Special Collections, The University of Texas at Arlington Libraries, Denton Record Chronicle, Denton County Office of History and Culture, Texas Observer, Zoe Rushing, Tom Sherrill, Shawn Palmer, and OOA Fonden - smilingsun.org

Visit the website at *jerrypalmerauthor.com*

115 Metroplex Blvd
Pearl, MS 39208
agpearl.com

Dedication

To Carobeth for her love

Lewis Pitts for his courage

Holly for her energy

The Coyotes (Kiotes) and all the eco-raiders of North America for their acts of justice

Shawn, Sara and Justin for my revival

The Yellow Rose Life Force for being

The Weather Underground for the past

Woodstock for paying it forward

Salvador Dali for drawing out time

Ken Nelson aka, Al Most, for propaganda by deed

Thank you to two true American Heroes, our Organizers: Mavis Belisle and Jim Schermbeck

Contents

Prologue vii

I	Occupation of June 10, 1979	1
II	Glen Rose Staging Area	13
III	June 10, 1979	21
IV	Trial of the 48	31
V	Occupation November 25, 1979 and the Yellow School Bus	55
VI	Winter 1979 to March 28, 1980 and the Road Gang	83
VII	Zoo World and The Pentagon 1980	105
VIII	Seabrook 1980 and The Eyes of Texas	131
IX	July 4, 1980	147
X	Making Our Presence Known	177
XI	Post Occupation Blues	185
XII	Diablo Canyon September 1981	191
XIII	Bringing the Battle to Them via The Paint Bucket Brigade	205
	Early June 2019, 40 years to the week	213

Epilogue 221

Profile or Comments from Contributors . . .223

**Song Written During
July 1980 Occupation** 233

Prologue

This book is an account of the Comanche Peak Life Force, a group of Texans and friends who acted in a way that was necessary and perhaps even revolutionary. People close to or involved in such actions should not judge this as a record. Instead consider it shared memories. For me, it sparks the fires of dissent that light the true torch of liberty in this land.

BLOW ON THIS DOT.

If It Turns Red, What The Govenment
& Utilities Tell You About
Nuclear Power, May Come True.

Such actions similar are part of a movement to speak out and resist social, economic, racial and environmental injustice in this country. We choose to march, stand, sit, climb, swim, barricade and pay heavy spiritual and monetary fines to protect ourselves, our descendants as well as the land, water, air, and natural resources of this semi-precious society so sweetly called western. Often in anger, but more often from the heart, banners are made, rallies held, picket lines walked, and barricades built. The true adventure was climbing the fence, cutting wire, camping on site and with helicopters overhead, knowing not to move other than to breathe. Camaraderie through affinity groups, co-ops, community gardens and direct action were the rewards then and now.

Two nuclear bombs detonated underground in Lamar County, Mississippi at the Tatum Salt Domes. That got my attention as a youngster living less than one hundred miles from the blast site. Project Salmon in October 1964 was a blast equivalent to 5,000 tons of TNT, about one-third as powerful as the bomb that destroyed Hiroshima in 1945. The other blast occurred in December 1966 with a force of 350 tons of TNT. These were the only nuclear explosions known to have occurred on United States soil east of the Rocky Mountains. The Tatum Salt Dome first made the local news as a necessary act of national security and patriotism, then as a site permanently contaminated with radioactivity. Now the site is open for public access. A granite monument surrounded by test wells mark the site of the nuclear bomb test. Don't play in the creek or drink the water.

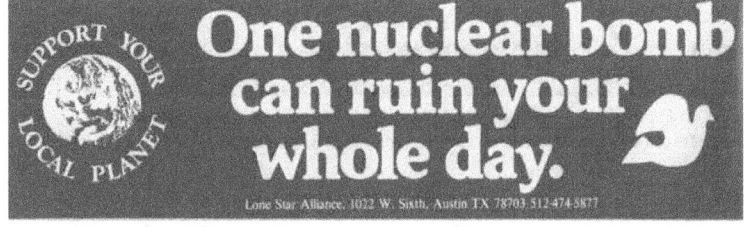

After spending two years on my aunts' farm in Dunn, Louisiana, I was raised in central Mississippi in the mid-

1950s and the early 1960s. The crowning of Mary Ann Mobley, a Brandon hometown girl as Miss America in 1959, the budding civil rights movement, and the start of American military involvement in Vietnam made for fertile  ground of the spirit (in action speaks louder than words) with this young white boy. A complete set of World Book Encyclopedia, with the annual yearbook delivered by the U.S. Postal Service, helped shape my view of the world.

My mom and dad moved to the farm in Rankin County in 1955, forty acres with a pond and five buildings constructed from trees cut from the property in the 1940s. A small house, barn, corn crib, chicken house (with electricity) and a one-seater outhouse. It had 35-foot well and a good woodlot to provide firewood, squirrels for food and plenty of room to discover the beauty and pitfalls of nature. My stepdad, Leon Bailey, worked for Mississippi Valley Gas Company in Jackson, and my mom, Wonize Juanita Bush, was a southern girl from Louisiana who raised a daughter and two more sons. Leon belonged to an independent union at the gas company and in the early 1960s they went on strike. He walked the picket lines, worked a stint offshore, and with the help of a mule-pulled set of plows farmed two garden plots for vegetables. One was a kitchen garden close to the house with the other larger plot east of the house near the barn. His commitment to his union brothers made a lasting impression on me about the meaning of solidarity. The union, after six long weeks on strike, won a nickel-an-hour raise and both sides were ready to get back to work.

The troubles in 1962, with James Meredith as the first African American to enroll at Ole Miss, caused quite a stir in predominantly white "good old boy" Mississippi. My dad refused a chance to go with our closest neighbor to help stop the perceived "commie threat" to our way of life. The neighbor owned and operated a bulldozer and road grader which he used to clear land and build ponds. His perennial source of income was doing work for a big shot lawyer in Brandon with a family history in politics going back generations and with strong ties to The White Citizens Council, now documented as a network of white supremacist, extreme right organizations in the South.

John F. Kennedy's assassination in 1963 affected the people around me differently. Some laughed and joked about the president's demise while others walked around with blank looks and hanging heads. The news of Medgar Evers' murder didn't make the headlines that I remember; I wasn't to learn of his murder until later. The integration of the public schools in Mississippi and the first wave of white flight to private and council schools made me realize that courage and cowardliness can drink from the same water fountain as well as eat from the same garden.

The daily body count of the dead and wounded in Vietnam shown on the nightly news was unforgettable. Protests of the United State's involvement were growing throughout the country. There was little or no sign of this in Mississippi until eleven days after the Ohio National Guard killed four

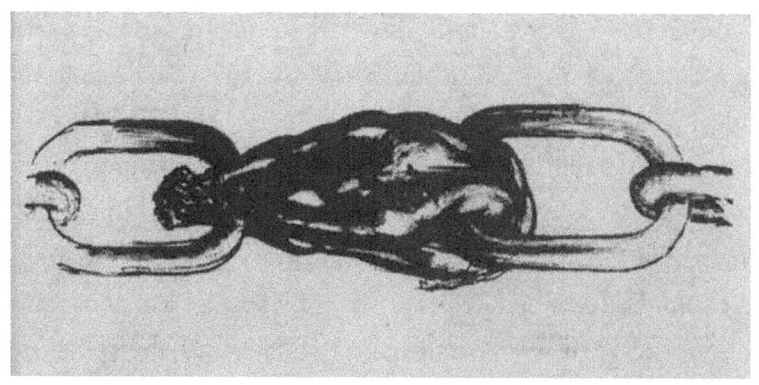

students at Kent State University. On Friday, May 15, 1970 the City of Jackson Police Department along with the Mississippi Highway Patrol confronted a group of students gathering at Jackson State College (now Jackson State University).

Jackson State College in 1970 had been the site of student unrest in support of the anti-Vietnam war movement across the country. A false rumor that another civil rights leader had been assassinated brought both high school and college students into the streets of Jackson. Lynch Street stretched right down the middle of campus, making it the perfect place for hot- headed rednecks and other southern patriots to hurl insults at students as they drove by. At about midnight on May 15, 1970, the JPD, a mostly white male force and the Mississippi National Guard arrived, and the terror began. Firing into the Alexander West Hall dormitory the police and National Guard killed two students and wounded a dozen more. The reasons for both the Kent State shootings and the shootings on the campus of Jackson State vary, depending on whom you ask, but I knew they were wrong in so many ways.

As a member of the football team at Hinds Junior College,

I didn't think much about how I could help make the world a better place. Saving the planet was a vague, yet compelling, idea. But news of canals up north catching fire due to industrial pollution and the Houston ship channel being declared dead from toxins from the petrochemical industry made me sad and angry, but I didn't know what, if anything, I could do about it. My curiosity grew when I learned more about the Earth Day event in April 1970, and about people trying to stop the slaughter of whales and the growing dead zone in the Gulf of Mexico due to pollution from the overuse of agricultural chemicals washed into the Mississippi River watershed then flushed downstream.

With friends from Vicksburg, I went to Jackson for adventure and ended up at the War Memorial Building. We

were all concerned about the war in Vietnam. Everybody knew a friend or relative who had been drafted or enlisted, who was missing in action, dead or came home forever changed. We all purchased nickel-plated prisoner of war commemorative bracelets with the rank, name, and loss date of an American servicemen captured or missing in the Vietnam War. That was the extent of my activism until I saw

a flyer on the bulletin board at a health food store in East Dallas. Join us in a No Nukes rally at Tarantula Ranch in Glen Rose, Texas June 2, 1979.

I moved to Dallas in the summer of 1975 and found work with a small landscape company. Later I moved to the larger well-known landscape firm, North Haven Gardens, where I learned some of the skills which I would later use as an arborist. Later I worked at Lambert's Landscape where I led a tree trimming crew in the more affluent sections of Dallas, Fort Worth and the Park Cities area. Working as a free agent arborist, I had time and resources and participate in the adventures ahead with the Comanche Peak Life Force.

I became a certified scuba diver and took an underwater archaeology class at Southern Methodist University taught by Dr. Joel Shiner, where I met open-minded adventurous people. Working on the first sanctioned underwater exploration of Aquarena Springs in San Marcos, Texas helped me understand that risky well-planned actions can often have positive results.

CHAPTER I
Occupation of June 10, 1979

A "No Nukes" rally was planned for June 2, 1979. Perhaps the people of Texas had finally decided to do something about the nuclear power plant cleverly named Comanche Peak Steam Electric Station. Perhaps they realized the time for direct action had arrived. Direct action often becomes necessary when other forms of protest such as writing letters, making phone calls, submitting petitions and debating doesn't bring about desired results. More visible militant action was required. Nonviolent civil disobedience has been used to affect social change for decades by the Women's Suffrage movement, Gandhi, the American Civil Rights movement, anti-war groups, environmental activists, and now the struggle against nuclear power and the call to dismantle all nuclear weapons.

Glen Rose, Texas, is about forty miles southwest of the Dallas-Fort Worth Metroplex. It is where Texas Utilities built their power plant. Being in a centralized spot helps the utility company make use of the electrical power grid, by using existing power for the construction and then send power out when construction is complete. Also, the lure of construction jobs is an easy selling point to the locals in this small rural country. I was working for a small tree service based in Granbury about fifteen miles north of Glen Rose and commuting 80 miles from Eastvale one way every day.

Curious about the rally and protest of the building of the nuclear plant, and eager to learn more about a planned protest/occupation at the nuke, I drove to Tarantula Ranch early in the morning on June 2, 1979. I found several hundred people, mostly young and middle-aged white folks. Yet one elderly couple with anti-nuke signs stood out; something about their resolve made me think this wasn't their first rodeo. Some parents with their kids were peacefully milling around, looking at literature, talking, glancing at an empty stage and buying t-shirts, buttons and bumper stickers (the big three in no-nuke fundraising). I was amazed at the large turnout of people and the organization of the rally so far from the big city. I bought a couple of bumper stickers, took a few pictures, then strolled over to my Datsun 280Z for a beer and a quick smoke. After listening to several musicians and speakers describe the dangers of nuclear

power and Comanche Peak in particular. When construction began in 1974, the estimated cost was $779 million. Fifteen years later it ballooned to over $9 billion.

The dangers of the plant range from the mining and milling uranium to the transporting of the fuel rods. It is dangerous primarily in terms of radiation exposure. Radioactive material is released from the plant into the environment. Such a release is usually characterized by a cloud-like plume of radioactive gases and particles. The major hazards to people and animals in the vicinity of the plume is the injection of radioactive material into the body from the cloud and particles in the air, then deposited on the ground, in the water and on vegetation. These issues along with the storage and disposal of the highly radioactive waste has been studied for years with no solution in sight. Yet profits from the nuclear power industry continue to drive investors in utility stocks cushioned by U.S. government subsidies since the Atoms for Peace program in the 1950s, to kick the can of nuclear waste down the road. While well-intentioned, the Atoms for Peace program has been criticized for facilitating nuclear proliferation by spreading dual use nuclear technology, i.e., technologies and materials, including highly-enriched uranium used in early civilian nuclear programs. Most nuclear waste from nuclear power plants is in the form of plutonium-239, one of the main components used in making nuclear weapons.

The leaflet the fellow with curly red hair handed me as I entered the rally, was titled Join us in Civil Disobedience on June 10 at Comanche Peak. Non-violence training required. The organizers'

intention to provide training encouraged me, and I believed some goodness would come of it. The non-violent civil disobedience training was scheduled the next day at a city park in Dallas. I was encouraged, but felt awkward as I didn't know a soul there.

The first training session seemed like a birthing class for this group of Dallas radicals, or so it seemed to me. This session was one of many being held around the state of Texas in preparation for the upcoming protest at Comanche Peak. Comanche Peak Life Force (CPLF) was formed in the spring of 1979 as an independent antinuclear group whose primary focus was using civil disobedience against nuclear power. Its founders were nuclear opponents in the Dallas-Fort Worth area who felt that resistance to the construction of the Comanche Peak nuclear power plant should be nonviolently escalated due to risks in its operation. Many members had been involved with a variety of other antinuclear groups and nonviolent protests against the plant including leafleting, picketing, petitioning and public education programs and the Life Force encouraged these means of dissent. The name Life Force is derived from a Gandhian term used to express the power of nonviolent action.

Twelve to 15 people showed up, ranging from older teenagers to folks in their forties, women and men in equal numbers. One couple brought their baby, which the mom carried in a harness on her chest. The dad was one of the trainers for this class. CPLF trainers learned their lessons and skills from the good folks from Oklahoma who were battling to stop the Black Fox nuclear plant.

Mavis Belisle, the meeting facilitator, arranged us in a circle in which we introduced ourselves and stated our reasons for being here. Trainers introduced us to consensus decision-making, which is a creative and dynamic way of reaching agreement among members of a group. Instead of simply voting and having the majority get their way, a group using consensus is committed to finding solutions that everyone actively supports, or can at least can live with. We also shared our reasons for being there and practiced role playing in different scenarios which might occur at the protest. The trainers were patient and understanding as they walked us through the process, and I began to feel a shared sense of purpose with the group. There was straight, heartfelt talk with no bullshit or sarcasm. A bit of humor made me feel at ease, and I soon recognized a kindred spirit and made a connection that has endured to the present.

The purpose of the protestors trespassing on private property was to put the nuclear power industry on public trial and to highlight pollution issues, long term health effects, as well as cost overruns. Those who chose to trespass would

COMANCHE PEAK LIFE FORCE

Occupation June 10

Because we believe the Comanche Peak nuclear power plant presents a clear and present danger to the health and safety of North Texas, we invite you to join us in a non-violent occupation of the site June 10.

Non-violence training required.
For information call 214-337-5885 or 817-534-3720

be arrested and brought to trial; this fact was made clear early, and it was stressed the action was a serious matter. Alternatives to nuclear power madness were also discussed, such as wind, solar and other renewable energy sources. We also discussed the threat we presented to the proponents of nuclear power and, finally, how the authorities might deal with us. The action on Sunday, June 10, 1979, was "greased" so there were no major issues in sight, but tear gas, dogs, horses, water cannons were discussed but lightheartedly. A greased action is one that the lawyers and legal aid for the protesters contact and inform the authorities of the upcoming actions. In the case of the CPLF, this was the Sheriff Frank Laramore of Somervell and the builders (Brown and Root Construction), owners of the Comanche Peak nuclear plant (Texas Utilities). This simple, but straight forward, approach gave clarity to the

authorities and expressed the peaceful nature of the protestors.

The organizers prepared a handbook, and it was required for everyone to read it. The meeting ended and we gathered for a group hug before heading home until we met again on Wednesday night in Garland. Other training classes had been held and more affinity groups around the state were making similar plans for the June 10 action.

People arrived at the next meeting, hugging old friends, smiling and greeting new ones. Food was brought for a pot-luck dinner (another identifying mark of the anti-nuke movement). There was a kettle of beans, casseroles, and homemade bread. The hostess made homemade pizza, but our most notable contribution was the twenty-dollar ham brought by an undercover police officer who could just as well have worn his badge on the outside of his polo shirt as he did his 14K gold necklace. My contribution to the spread was two delicious Pecos cantaloupes that went faster than a joint in a room of Rastas.

In the front yard lay a sturdy wooden homemade ladder. A statement of sincerity and determination, it was also a tool to build trust and camaraderie. The ladder, with the final touches put on it, was more of a stile to be used to cross the fence at Comanche Peak. We practiced climbing the five sturdy two-by-four steps and jumping to the ground several times.

We silkscreened red t-shirts designed with twin domes and a slash circle around them, along with the date and group name. Once the ink on the shirts were dry, we were instructed to wash them once to set the silkscreen design into the fabric.

Before the meeting ended, the organizers of the Life Force made sure the people who were to be arrested during the protest filled out legal cards. Supporters (non-fence jumpers) were also asked questions about their medical history and contact phone numbers.

All this was previously decided on and set into action by the organizers of the Life Force, with the help of lawyers and activists from earlier actions, namely the Clamshell Alliance fighting the Seabrook nuclear power plant in New

> Recognizing the necessity of nonviolence in civil disobedience actions, and my own responsibility to my sisters and brothers in Comanche Peak Life Force, I offer my pledge that:
>
> My attitude will be one of openness, friendliness and respect toward all people we encounter;
> I will use no physical or verbal violence toward any person;
> I have received training in nonviolence;
> I will not damage any property;
> I will not bring weapons of any kind onto the campground or occupation site;
> I will bring no alcohol or illegal drugs onto the campsite or occupation site;
> I will not run at any time;
> I will not block workers' personal access to the site, or interfere with their work;
> I will not bring dogs or other animals onto the occupation site;
> I will not attempt to break through police lines;
> I will not engage in tactical or strategic movements on the occupation site during darkness.
>
> I recognize that any violation of the code that results in increased danger or legal jeopardy for other members of Comanche Peak Life Force will result in my disaffiliation from the group, and that members of the Life Force will assist with prosecution for any violation that involves additional legal prosecution.
>
> _____
> signature
>
> _____
> affinity group

Hampshire, and those from Oklahoma working against the Black Fox nuclear plant - the construction of which was later cancelled.

Some had political ambitions which unfolded in the future. Given time and their actions, fruitful or not, these folks were some of the American patriots of the late twentieth century. We formed a circle and had a group hug before separating until Saturday afternoon in Glen Rose, Texas at T's place, which would serve as our staging area.

"T" was a local fellow, who, for his own reasons, disapproved of the nuclear plant being built in his part of Texas and offered his place to be used as a base camp, or staging area, for the protest. This location was perfect in hindsight since it was only a couple of blocks away from the Somervell County courthouse where the trials of those arrested would take place.

Comanche Peak Steam Electric Station

Electricity for progress with nuclear power.

Nuclear Steam Supply

The basic difference between a fossil fuel power plant and a nuclear power plant is the source of heat used to produce steam.

In a fossil fuel power plant, coal, oil or gas is burned in a boiler provides heat to change water to steam. The steam turns the blades of a turbine which spins a generator, producing electricity. In a nuclear plant, the boiler is replaced by a reactor containing a core of nuclear fuel.

Safety

Nuclear power plants are designed, built and operated with overriding concern for public safety. They must conform to the most stringent safety standards, including multiple safety protection systems, and are built to withstand natural disasters (such as earthquakes and tornadoes) or the worst accidents the experts have been able to imagine (like an airplane crash) without harm to the public.

No member of the public has ever been injured (much less killed) as the result of an accident involving a commercial U.S. nuclear power plant. That remarkable safety record covers about 500 reactor-years of operation.

Radiation

Radiation is measured in units called millirems, and people in this area usually receive about 100 millirems of radiation a year from natural sources. The radiation comes from outer space, from the ground, from what we eat and drink, from building materials, and from other sources.

The Comanche Peak plant is designed to limit radiation releases to less than one millirem per year, far below natural levels. A typical tooth X-ray would subject you to as much radiation as living 100 years next to a nuclear power plant.

Waste handling and storage

No power plant employee has ever suffered a radiation injury as a result of handling waste, and no one has received a radiation injury through the transportation of waste.

The federal government has taken responsibility for the disposal of waste materials and the handling of used fuel (commonly referred to as spent fuel). Used fuel will be temporarily stored at the plant site before it is delivered to a federal facility.

The U.S. Department of Energy is now developing plans for the safe, permanent disposal of radioactive waste products.

Dallas Power & Light Company
Texas Electric Service Company
Texas Power & Light Company

Why nuclear power?

Today, natural gas is the main fuel used for making electricity in Texas. But natural gas has become very expensive, and new long-term supplies to meet future needs are not available. Besides, both gas and oil should be preserved for use where alternate fuels are not available. The only other fuels that can meet our needs for electricity in coming years are coal and nuclear fuel.

Dallas Power and Light Co., Texas Electric Service Co. and Texas Power and Light Co. are using reserves of lignite coal in East Texas to make electricity. This lignite, acquired years ago, costs much less than new supplies of gas or oil.

But even these large lignite reserves will not be sufficient to meet all of the area's future needs for electricity. So the three companies are building the Comanche Peak nuclear power plant near Glen Rose. It will begin producing power near the time that several major natural gas supply contracts expire.

Plants that use lignite coal or nuclear fuel cost much more to build than gas-fueled plants. This means the price of electricity must go up in the future. But it would go up even higher if we tried to rely on gas and oil as fuel.

Facts about Comanche Peak steam electric station

Status

Construction of the Comanche Peak plant began in late 1974, after more than four years of comprehensive research and planning. A construction permit was issued by the Atomic Energy Commission (now the Nuclear Regulatory Commission) only after volumes of evidence had been studied and public hearings had been held on the environmental and safety aspects of the plant.

The first unit at the plant is to be completed in 1981, and the second in 1983. When completed, the plant will have a capacity of 2,300,000 kilowatts, which is about the capacity needed to supply electricity to a city one and one-half times the size of Fort Worth. Employment during construction will average about 1,500 workers.

Location

Plant location is in Somervell County, about five miles north of Glen Rose.

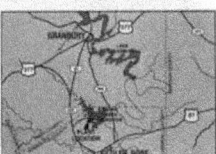

Reservoir

The 3,300-acre Squaw Creek Reservoir (volume: 151,000 acre-feet) will supply the plant with condenser cooling water. Plans are that the lake and the shoreline will be available for recreational uses. Filling of the reservoir began Feb. 15, 1977 and was completed in May 1979.

Fuel

The fuel is in the form of uranium dioxide pellets with about three percent Uranium 235 enrichment. Each pellet will supply about the same heat energy as a ton of coal.

Reactor vessel

Each of the two carbon steel reactor vessels will hold a fuel core. Each is 43 feet, 10 inches tall, 157 inches in diameter, and weighs 450 tons.

Containment buildings

These structures house the reactor systems. Each will be 265 feet tall with an inside diameter of 135 feet. They have a wall thickness of 4½ feet and their foundations are 12 feet thick.

Principal contractors
Architect-engineer: Gibbs & Hill
General contractor: Brown & Root
Environmental studies: Dames & Moore
Reactors: Westinghouse
Turbine-generators: Allis-Chalmers

Facts about nuclear power

Economics

Because of the relatively low fuel cost, electricity from the Comanche Peak plant will cost less than electricity from a plant burning high-priced gas or oil.

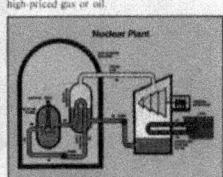

CHAPTER II
Glen Rose Staging Area

I arrived early on June 9 to T's place, a two-acre lot surrounded on two sides with a cedar post fence resembling a stockade. The south side of the property was open to a small two-lane street. The north side gently sloped down to the Paluxy River, where a sweat lodge was being constructed. An early twentieth century wood framed house stood on the southwestern corner and a faded yellow mobile home occupied the northeastern corner. The structures served as sign-in points and places to gather if the weather turned bad. I brought only a day-glow orange backpack with a change of clothes inside.  I drove around waiting for more cars to show, taking some time to look around this quaint Texas town. By the time I returned, T's place was humming with activity and the neighbors looked concerned.

In no time, the encampment, which included the trailer and small house, began to look like a small fort. It was a sight to see. Mountain cedar poles roughly three to four inches in diameter and six or seven feet tall, had been placed

upright and wired so close together mosquitos had a hard time getting between them. Cars and a few trucks lined the roadside ditch and scores of people came and went carrying tents and camping gear. After reading a list of guidelines nailed to the fence, I truly began to believe something could be done to stop the nuke, or at least slow the construction progress.

The affinity groups began to set up camp for the night. Affinity groups consisted of anywhere between eight to twenty people banded together by location, friendship, or true affinity for a purpose, goal or cause. Affinity groups date back to the Spanish Civil War, or further back by nomadic bands who roamed this continent since before written record. The Dallas group was scattered all about, working the sign-in at the gate, outside security, and some were preparing for the last non-violence training before the action tomorrow. Affinity groups from Austin, Denton, Fort Worth, Houston and other parts of Texas and Oklahoma were in attendance. Communication by phone, letters, and personal contacts help keep everyone in the loop.

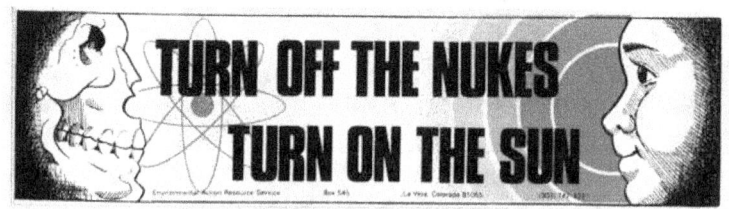

I scoped out a group of hackberry trees on the west side of the property that looked like an ideal spot to hang my hammock. As darkness began to settle over the encampment,

I took notice of the dozens of people camped out. Some were in nice tents, while others slept in home-made lean-to shelters. By my estimate we numbered around a hundred souls.

Excitement filled the air, I thought perhaps the numbers would grow and we could at last rid Texas of the nuke. The comfort of caring for something more than myself, and acting on it, began to settle in my soul. When it started raining, I moved from my hammock to my car, which was parked in the ditch outside the fence. The night passed into morning and the spirit of excitement grew along with our numbers. A mutual feeling of power in the people began to encircle all of us. Friendships were made, and chants and prayers were said, as we prepared to caravan to the plant site.

After the camp kitchen volunteers served a breakfast of natural oatmeal, fruit and a salad made of sprouts, along with plenty of hot coffee, a spirit of community washed over me. I felt as though my thirst for action had been quenched from the Edwards Aquifer, one of the most prolific artesian aquifers in the world that lay deep under our feet. Prior planning was important, as making decisions by consensus takes more time, but the returns are far greater than when the majority rules. This may not be a long-term solution, but there is a taste of personal freedom when it takes place.

Everyone there honestly cared for the Earth, and each stood to be counted as we prepared to march against the power of the atom- or power of the dollar- according to the views of each person.

Stepping onto an drink cooler to take a photo for future reference, I noticed the stern looks and the serious nature of the folks around me. Had they been to occupations before and realized that trouble or unforeseen problems lay only moments away? Or was I so busy checking out this group I had missed a warning? I felt confident about what was about to take place, but with reservations. I still wanted to be counted in the numbers of those climbing over the fence, knowing that was breaking the law by committing criminal trespass, therefore putting nuclear power on trial with the aid of supporters, lawyers and ladders.

As many more actions and occupations developed around the country, I felt empowered, along with others, to try and stop the nukes. Occupations are a term given to the action of being on utility or nuclear facility property illegally for some length of time. Many already knew these acts of duress and necessity were symbolic. The utility companies across the country, including Texas Electric Utilities, Con Edison (one of the largest investor-owned energy companies in the United States), Brown and Root or Pacific Gas and Electric had recently dealt with the proverbial thorn (constant protests) in

their sides. Their problems were cost overruns, construction problems (cracks in the domes) and not knowing what in the hell to do with the spent fuel rods (nuclear waste) other than store them onsite. They played a musical chairs type of waste dump game waiting on the Federal archangel to say where it was to lay forever.

A wide-open area in the compound allowed the group to form a large circle. Joining these volunteers, I watched as others grasped hands, arms and shoulders. The spirit and power of numbers greater than one left an impression on me for years afterward. A count began and continued around the circle until we numbered one hundred and eight strong. Forty-eight to cross their lines and with sixty more in support. The circle broke and we began to fill cars, trucks and vans that would carry us to the nuclear site and into Texas history.

CHAPTER III
June 10, 1979

After a ten-minute ride north on Hwy 56 the domes of the still under construction Comanche Peak Nuclear Power Plant came into sight and then disappeared behind a mesa of cedars, scrub live oaks and mesquite trees. Turning onto a road with a large field and several side roads with a barbed wire fence on the east side, we stopped and slowly exited the vehicles. Everyone formed a line that seemed to have several hundred people, for our numbers had increased during the drive over as more people joined our motorcade. The Texas press  was in attendance along with many supporters and observers. The June 10, 1979 Occupation of Comanche Peak had been well publicized ahead of time.

As we waited, we unfurled banners and American flags, some folks shouting with dissent. As if on command there was a wave of red t-shirts, black armbands and backpacks, marching in unison to the fence. As we turned onto the main road (United Way Drive) chants of "No Nukes—No Nukes!"

filled the air. Some sang a chorus of Like A Tree Standing by The Waters, which rang loud and true during the march. Once we reached the four-foot wire fence, I couldn't help but notice the white pickups and sedans accompanied by fellows wearing white hard hats and sporting sunglasses. Just beyond the trucks were yellow school buses blocking the road, several yards behind the locked gate.

"If you cross the fence, you will be arrested for trespassing on private property," the lanky cowboy-dressed Sheriff Laramore announced. He was at ease, and rightly so. This was a plan greased well ahead of time with the local authorities. It was a situation where people were intentionally breaking the law and the Comanche Peak Life Force, though our legal team, told the Sheriff about it. He knew when, where, and how the protest would happen and all he had to do was provide transportation to the jail. The utility company helped with

this task by providing buses. The Somervell County Jail in Glen Rose was another story as it had only two holding cells, and one of those was used to store the Sheriff's campaign materials, old coffee pots and such.

Taking notice and purposely hanging back a little as volunteers began to cross the fence, I was about the seventh or eighth person in line. What I observed was a phenomenon known as "sheep to slaughter" in anti-nuclear circles. Here we were, 48 protesters, nearly running to get arrested, to board the bus to Glen Rose. If not for the press, whose presence nearly outnumbered the county law enforcement officers, I had to wonder if the action served much more than a steppingstone to the next protest of the Life Force. The local media, along

with independent filmmakers, recorded the wonderfully choreographed first-of-its-kind act of civil disobedience in Texas against nuclear power. The focus was to bring attention and public awareness to the immediate and long-term issues of the nuclear power industry. From the mining of uranium

Protester climbs fence Sunday at Comanche Peak

Somervell County Sheriff Frank Laramore escorts protesters to bus for trip to j[ail]

...sted in Glen Rose nuclear protest

Both sides are satisfied with results

Somervell County Sheriff Frank Laramore escorts protesters to bus for trip to jail

on Indian Nation land to the transportation and storage of the highly toxic radioactive waste produced in research facilities and nuclear powered steam electric plants, I realized this was where a public trial with a jury would come into play.

After crossing the fence, some affinity groups sat in circles, holding aloft American and Texas flags, while others were

celebrating by sharing hugs and handshakes with supporters on the safe side of the fence. With reporters and cameramen on the occupied side, interviews with Sherriff Laramore took place while the spirit of this action spread among us. Then after this short reprieve we were asked to stand and then

were led without handcuffs or restraints to the two awaiting school buses. The songs and chanting along with the cheers from spectators filled the air as we were driven back to Glen Rose as the first arrested civil disobedience protestors at a nuclear power plant in Texas.

As the yellow school buses pulled up to the small three-story stone jail in Glen Rose, it occurred to me the ride back to town took longer than the fence jumping act of civil disobedience. After presenting identification and signing the citation for criminal trespassing of which one copy stayed with the sheriff's office and one copy was given to each protester arrested, we were released on our personal recognizance. We regrouped at our encampment overlooking the Paluxy River, about a three-block walk from the jail. With citations held like badges of courage and wearing smiles that would light the future, hugs, handshakes and even a few tears were shared throughout the camp. Feeling like a young hawk just

```
                    TOMMY ALTARAS
                     ATTORNEY AT LAW
                  Third Floor Johnson County Courthouse
                       Cleburne, Texas 76031
                         Phone: 641-5310

                        October 17, 1979


       Gerald Wayne Palmer
       Route 3, Box 290
       Lewisville, TX  75056



                              RE:  State of Texas
                                   vs.
                                   Gerald Wayne Palmer
                                   (Criminal Trespass,
                                   Somervell County, TX)
       Dear Mr. Palmer:

               You have been charged with criminal trespass.
       You are to appear in the Somervell County Court,
       Glen Rose, Texas, on November 2, 1979 at 9:00 A.M.
       for pre-trial.

               You must have your attorney present in court
       with you.

                              Very truly yours,


                              TOMMY ALTARAS
                              Special Prosecutor

       TA:mw
       cc:  Mr. Tom Mills
            One Turtle Creek Village
            3800 Oak Lawn
            Dallas, TX  75219

            Mr. Charles Jordan
            Somervell County Courthouse
            Glen Rose, TX  76043
```

pushed from the nest, I was ready to do more against the proliferation of nuclear power and promote safe renewable energy. Not sure exactly what to do, I did feel stronger and full of courage to continue in this struggle for a clean and safe environment. I decided of educate myself in layman terms about the process of boiling water with uranium 235 to make steam for turning turbines. Reading as much about the trail of uranium ore (yellowcake) to the result of plutonium 239 with a half-life of 24,000 years began a mission and served to harden my resolve against the nuclear industry.

The first step now for CPLF trespassers was to await the date of the pretrial hearing. We were to be notified by mail. We received our notices, first for the hearing, then for the trial, all of which was set to begin the last week of June 1979 at the Somervell County Courthouse in beautiful downtown Glen Rose, Texas.

CHAPTER IV
Trial of the 48

Tom Mills of Dallas and the honorable Lewis Pitts of North Carolina provided legal defense for the defendants' pro bono. Pitts was permitted to practice law in the court of County Judge Sam Freas, even though he wasn't a member of the Texas Bar Association, since he was working with Tom Mills, an able orator in his own right and true Texan.

The trial took three days and at times felt like a camp revival. Other times there was a sense of hopelessness of fighting a mega-giant of an industry with roots in all the industrialized nations.

We were tried as a group, just one case. Our defense was "duress" and "necessity," which in Texas allows a person to act if they sense danger rather than wait until danger is upon them. With resources that amazed everyone, expert witnesses were brought in from Pittsburgh and New York, testifying that the Comanche Peak Steam Electric Plant was potentially dangerous to the people and life in North Texas area. Dr. Ernest Sternglass and Dr. Rosalie Bertell both deserved more respect than what they received from the county attorney and deserve high praise for time and sacrifices made in order to spread their knowledge about the dangers of nuclear power and the real cost involved in their mishandling. The expense of bringing these expert witnesses in for their testimonies were covered by the members of the Comanche Peak Life Force.

Judge Freas ordered the jury to consider the testimony of the two witnesses and to consider the unusual defense of "duress and necessity." After six hours of deliberating, the jury was deadlocked and a mistrial was declared at 11:30 pm. The jury was divided four for two against

acquittal. The two who voted guilty had sons who worked at the plant. As reported in the Fort Worth-Dallas area newspapers, the jurors openly remarked that the revelation heard in court had changed their minds in regard to the fact that the protestors were serious and that Comanche Peak Electric Station was indeed a threat to be dealt with. One even mentioned if he had known beforehand what was reported and verified by Dr. Sternglass and Dr. Bertell, he, too, may have climbed over the fence alongside the protestors. We took the decision of acquittal as a victory, which it truly was, for we sure as hell jumped that fence. Years later I still feel the necessity of acting in defense of our children and the environment.

Jim Schermbeck: An Answer from the Village Square
(Written in late June 1979)

Glen Rose is a small town in small Somervell County, Texas, 35 miles from the edge of the Fort Worth-Dallas "metroplex". It sits along the banks of the Paluxy River and among some of the most beautiful hill country north of Austin. One of hundreds of Texas hamlets you find once you get off the interstates, Glen Rose features a three-story courthouse that sits in the middle of the town square, surrounded by small shops and old-timers. For years Glen Rose was best known for its above-average moonshine (thanks to the local springs) and the dinosaur tracks which are scattered across the limestone formations by the river. In many respects the town is typical of the fast disappearing rural tradition of Texas—except that in two years it was due to have an operating nuclear power plant as a neighbor.

Just five miles north of Glen Rose, Texas Utilities was in its fifth year of construction of the Comanche Peak "Steam Electric Station," the Comanche Peak

Somervell County
Glen Rose, Texas

"To the village square we must carry the facts about atomic energy. From there must come America's voice." A. Einstein

Nuclear Power Plant, which is replacing the town's older landmarks with two 265-foot domes that tower above the landscape. The plant was designed to house two Westinghouse 1150 megawatt nuclear reactors and more radioactive materials than 2000 Hiroshima-size bombs.

Five years into the construction, the plant (named after a local plateau used as a meeting place by Indians and settlers) represented an economic boom to Glen Rose. Restaurants and businesses in the community have never been busier, supplying the needs of some 4000 construction workers at the plant. The county tax rolls have also benefited, collecting from a facility which was originally estimated at $777 million but is now costing ratepayers (all of whom live outside Glen Rose since the town's electrical coop did not buy into the plant) $2 billion—not including transmission, decommissioning or waste disposal cost. Many local farmers and ranchers supplemented their incomes by finding part time work at the plant and most of the county's young people had secure summer jobs there. The pay was good, and the qualifications are secondary since the contractor doing the construction work—Brown and Root (of tiger-cage fame), never hired union help.

For many years, antinuclear activists from the Fort Worth-Dallas area have been trying to mount a movement against the plant from within the town's ranks, but with little success. The economic incentives the plant offered, if only temporary, and the suspicions the townspeople had about "outsiders" built a formidable wall to effective organizing from the urban areas. But perhaps more serious, the activists themselves fell into stereotyping the townsfolk as 'redneck' and for the most part wrote off the community as too conservative to organize. However, they went out of their way to avoid offending the town by dismissing such strategies as civil disobedience, and in effect let their attitudes about what they thought Glen Rose would and would not tolerate guide their actions. It was feared that by breaking the law, even in a nonviolent and disciplined manner, they would alienate the town even more, even though no act of civil disobedience had ever been used against a Texas nuke. (Besides Comanche Peak, which is due online in 1981, there is the South Texas Nuclear Project, being built on the coast about 60 miles southwest of Houston, which is to begin operation sometime in the mid-80's.)

Combine the jobs, the tax rolls and the five-year momentum the plant has rolled up, and one might indeed believe that you have an unlikely chance of finding sympathy in Glen Rose for those who would openly and defiantly break the law in order to protest Comanche Peak. But this was not the case.

In fact, it is ironic that it took the most militant act of protest against Comanche Peak to date to win one of the most significant grassroots victories for the

Texas antinuclear movement. On June 30, four out of six Glen Rose residents on a jury voted to acquit 48 people of trespassing charges, thereby forcing a mistrial in the case. The 48 had climbed over a fence onto utility property at the Comanche Peak plant and occupied a portion of the site 20 days earlier. The four jurors voted for acquittal because they believed the 48 were justified in committing trespass due to the hazards posed by the nuclear plant.

The mistrial was an important step in fighting the utility on what had been taken for granted as pro-nuke territory. But the event is also important from a strategic standpoint in that it resulted in a vindication of civil disobedience from the grassroots level and highlighted the importance trials can have after occupations in winning the nuke debate within local communities.

The trial was the climax of a series of events that began in early May with the formation of the Comanche Peak Life Force. The group announced it was going to nonviolently "occupy" the Comanche Peak plant on June 10 in support of the International Days of Protest against nuclear power.

Between May 8 and June 10, the Life Force trained some 100 people in nonviolence, most from the Dallas-Fort Worth area, but also folks from Austin and around Glen Rose. Life Force members spoke to Glen Rose property owners and arranged for a June 9 campsite in a lot almost in the middle of town. They also spoke to the Somervell County sheriff and were assured that if the occupation were nonviolent, the authorities' response would be also.

On June 10, 1979, 48 "Lifers," supported by some 60 other trained members and friends and about 100 unexpected spectators, climbed over the fence at Comanche Peak. They walked about 15 yards onto plant property and then were stopped by a police line. All 48 sat and remained on site for 20 minutes before being arrested and escorted to waiting buses. They were driven back to Glen Rose, booked on trespassing charges and then released on personal recognizance. It had been agreed that everyone would plead not guilty, thereby forcing a trial within 30 days under the Texas speedy trial act.

The trial date was set for June 27 and between the occupation and that time, Life Force attorneys laid the foundation for what they hoped would be a chance to put nuclear power on trial. They planned to base the Life Force case on the defenses of "necessity" and "duress," which under Texas law can excuse someone from committing a crime because of "force or threat of force" or if the crime committed is less harmful than the object of the violator's actions, then she/he must be found not guilty. The force or threat of force must be such that a person of "reasonable firmness" would be frightened enough to act.

To help prove that Comanche Peak was such a threat, the attorneys arranged to have Dr. Rosalie

Bertell and Dr. Ernest Sternglass testify as expert witnesses about the dangers of nuclear power. The two are well-known scientists who had experience in testifying at occupation trials.

The attorneys also met with both the county judge and county prosecutor to explain the Life Force's defense. They are the only attorneys in the all of Somervell County, but the Life Force was going to be the judge's first jury trial and he had to borrow a gavel and a court reporter from an adjacent county.

The scene ,and often the mood, of the trial was right out of the classic 1960 film Inherit the Wind. The courthouse has only one small courtroom and the building's only bathrooms are outside. During testimony, the air conditioners had to be turned off because they were so loud, forcing everyone to shed coats, loosen ties and get out their hand fans. The room was always packed, and with the television cameras and newspaper reporters, it could have easily turned into a circus.

But the trial turned out to be a dramatic confrontation between the county prosecutor, who claimed the 48 defendants were "usurping the democratic process" and the defense, which argued the occupiers represented the conscience of that process.

On the first day of the trial, however, it was clear who was usurping what. Jury selection, which was expected to run an hour at most, took four hours.

Most of the time was spent preventing the prosecutor from sabotaging the trial altogether. He claimed that the state had a potential 144 jury strikes since the law normally allows three in a case involving one defendant, and this one had 48. He argued that he had the option of dismissing the entire jury panel of 40 that had shown up at the courthouse. The justification for that dismissal, he said, was the defendants' "right to a fair trial" which he claimed was impossible in Glen Rose since all the potential jurors indicated they had seen the defendants climb the utility's fence either on television or in photos from Fort Worth or Dallas newspapers and thereby commit an act of trespass. The prosecutor didn't mention in his request for dismissal that the defense was not contesting the act of trespassing but offering legal justification for it. It took the defense attorneys

to ask the panel if they could listen fairly to both sides and reserve a final opinion until after they had heard all the testimony—half said they could. The defense then pleaded with the judge to continue the trial in Glen Rose, that it was where the defendants wanted it and where they believed they could get the fair trial the prosecutor seemed to desire.

The judge, after some questions to the jury of his own, decided to limit the prosecutor to three strikes and granted the defense as many as was necessary to trim the number of remaining panel members to the six required for the trial to proceed.

Although the prosecutor's dismissal motion caught everyone off guard it should have been no surprise to see the state attempt to move the trial out of Glen Rose, perhaps to another town not so intimate with Comanche Peak. The embarrassment of an acquittal or hung jury in this case was probably a strong motivation in seeking a change in venue.

Among the four men and two women finally chosen to sit in judgment of the occupiers was the wife of a Baptist minister, a part-time hog farmer and, appropriately enough, a peanut farmer. Four of the six had raised their hands earlier when the prosecutor asked if they thought the defendants were guilty of trespassing. From their looks it was hard to imagine six more rural, white middle class citizens and more than one defendant stating that if there was a challenge to the power and truth of their arguments, this jury would be it.

The State had only one witness, Sheriff Frank Laramore, who testified that the defendants had climbed over the fence in question on June 10, 1979, were arrested, booked on trespassing charges and released on the same day. On cross examination the sheriff turned out to be the defense's best witness on the nonviolent character of the occupation. He confirmed that there had been no one hurt, and no property damaged. Asked if the occupation had any negative effects as far as he was concerned, Laramore jokingly replied that it had only "ruined" his Sunday.

It was clear from his attitude on the stand that the Sheriff could not have cared less if the defendants were convicted, that he was doing his job and it was the utility company that was complaining about the defendants, not him.

The prosecutor, however called no one from Texas Utilities and after the Sheriff's testimony, rested the State's case. In fact, Texas Utilities was to be conspicuous by its absence. As far as anyone could tell they didn't even send an observer to the trial.

The defense attorneys immediately began to build their "duress" and "necessity" defenses. The first of six representative defendants who would testify on behalf of the entire Life Force took the stand and related why he felt compelled to occupy Comanche Peak. His testimony and that of the five "spokes" spread over the entire three-day period laid a foundation for the appearances of Dr. Bertell and Dr. Sternglass. All six told of their frustration with trying to work within "the system" to stop the plant and why they believed occupying it was a reasonable action to take. "There are only so many petitions you can sign, only so many people you can talk to, only so many leaflets you can hand out making you realize it's going to take more to stop this plant and nuclear power," said one. Another defendant, a pregnant mother, related how her fear for her unborn baby prompted her to occupy and that even though she lived 150 miles from the plant, Comanche Peak was still "too close."

A Dallas nun testified that she felt it was a "moral imperative" to occupy, to stop work on an "immoral energy source." At the end of their collective testimony on Friday, the spokes had presented powerful and painfully sincere cases for their actions based on a real fear for lives and property. In effect, they were meeting the duress and necessity statutes by arguing that they felt compelled to occupy in light of their knowledge of nuclear power and that the occupation was necessary in the face of great harms the Comanche Peak plant would be producing.

The prosecutor, however, was not convinced the courtroom was the place to debate nuclear energy and for the first two days of defense testimony he constantly objected to the introduction of the duress and necessity defenses. At one point he objected ten

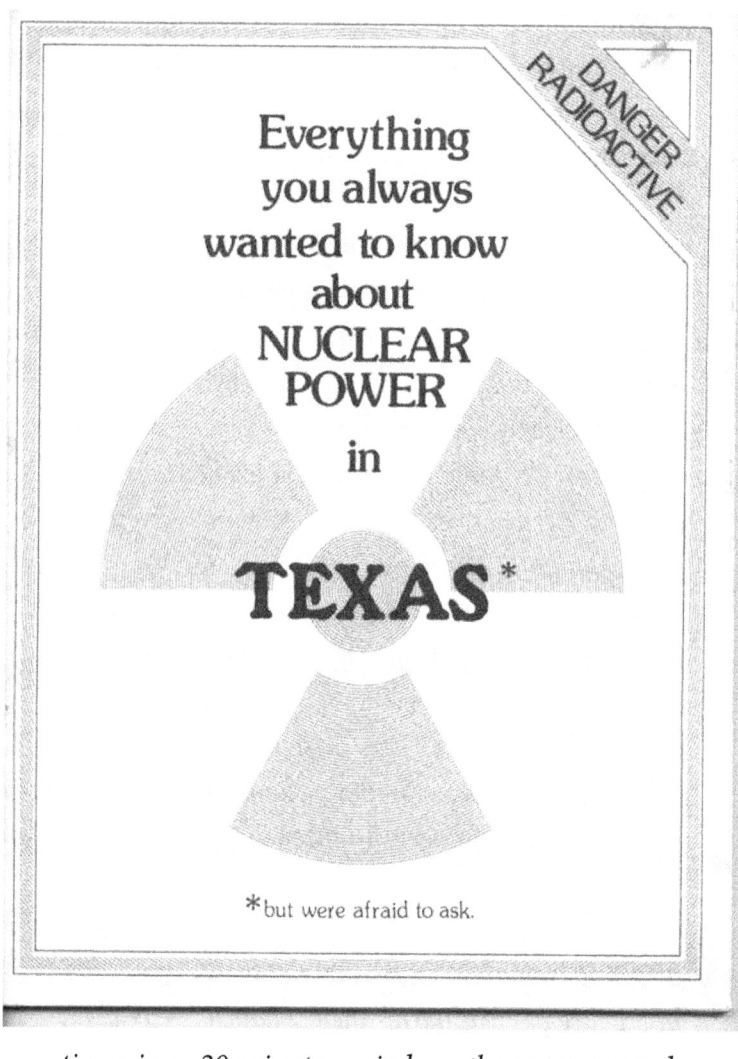

times in a 20-minute period on the same grounds of irrelevancy. The judge responded almost every time with the same answer, he would take the prosecutor's objections under advisement and rule on the appropriateness of the defenses at the end of testimony. Meanwhile, the defense would be permitted to call all of its witnesses and both the judge and jury would hear all the testimony.

The trial reached a dramatic climax on the second day with the appearances of Dr. Bertell and Dr. Sternglass. It was their expert testimony that gave new significance and credibility to the spokes' stated fears and the defendant's action.

Dr. Bertell was first, and she clearly impressed both the judge and jury with her qualifications and the detailed knowledge of radiation and its effects. As she methodically described how radioactivity can impact human health and the environment the entire courtroom listened with newfound attentiveness.

Under questioning from the defense attorneys, she testified that radiation is routinely released from all nuclear power plants and can contaminate areas many miles from the plants themselves, even in normal operation. "Radioactive ions are not as big as bullets, but they follow the same principle," she explained. "They are a threat to health and the food supply and there is no question that such radiation will be released from Comanche Peak."

Dr. Bertell stated that the limits the federal government maintains on such emissions are ten to twenty times too high and that, in fact, there is no known amount of radiation that won't cause harm. Describing radiation as a "force," Dr. Bertell stated that a person of reasonable firmness would be justified in fearing nuclear power.

Dr. Sternglass was next and gave the most emotional plea to close the nuclear industry the courtroom had heard. In a style which often resembled that of a country preacher, Sternglass foretold of death and disease in Glen Rose if Comanche Peak should open. He related grim statistics from his studies of some communities in the United States which already have nukes as neighbors: 50% increases in other diseases caused by radiation that could be traced to nowhere but nuclear plants.

Almost shouting at times, Sternglass conveyed a strong sense of fear, anger and bitterness toward the nuclear industry, for which he had worked for 18 years before discovering that nuclear plants "produce something which is very harmful."

"These radioactive ions released by nuclear plants are just like tiny x-ray machines sitting in your bones," he said. "But it is engineeringly impossible to build a plant that won't release radiation." He concluded his testimony by stating that "radioactivity is a force of nature, a force that strikes the body," and that a person of reasonable firmness "should be frightened about nuclear energy." Sternglass delivered a presentation that electrified the courtroom and, with Dr. Rosalie Bertells testimony, was invaluable to the defendants' case. Their appearances were, by all accounts the turning point in the trial. The media, spectators, judge and jury realized that the stakes had been upped considerably by the facts they had presented. Nuclear power was now being put on trial.

The prosecutor, who had again attempted to interrupt the flow of the defendant's case earlier in the morning, sat quietly in his chair for most of the rest of the trial and asked only token questions of Dr. Bertell and Dr. Sternglass. In fact, the last three defendants testifying on Friday were not cross examined at

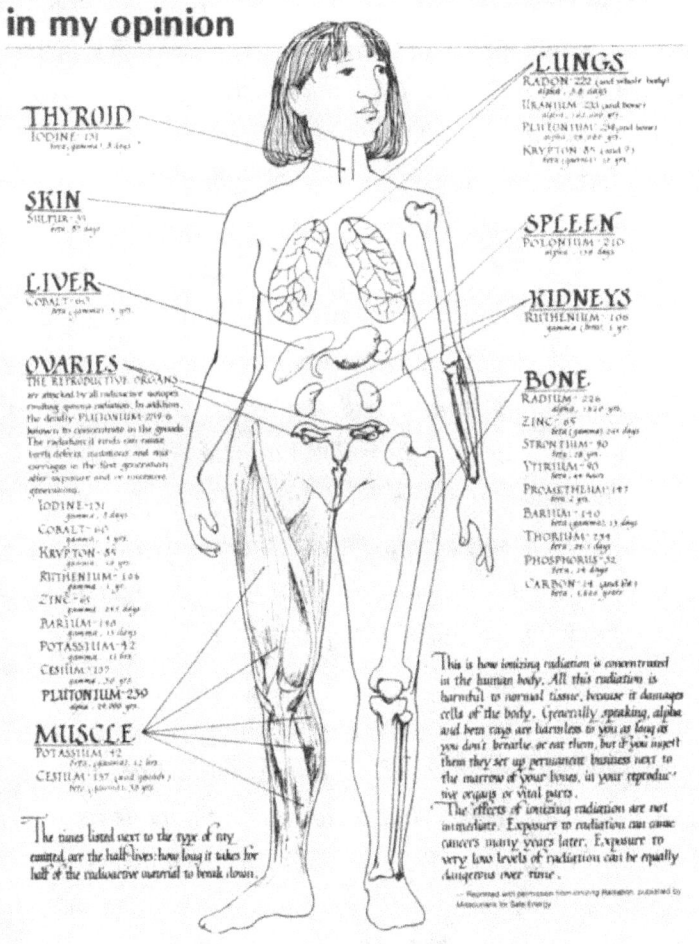

all. It appeared he was resigned to the fact that the Comanche Peak plant as well as the defendants was being judged by the jury.

On the third, and final, day of the trial, the judge handed the defendants a major victory when he ruled that the defenses of duress and necessity would be admitted, and the jury was instructed to consider them in reaching a verdict. The prosecutor was, of course, disappointed, having argued for the entire course of the trial that such defenses were inappropriate to the charges of trespassing. But the judge, persuaded by the spokes and the expert witnesses, stated that the link of danger and "threat of force" to the defendants' actions had been shown. However, this ruling came on the heels of a decision by the judge not to allow testimony about alternative energy sources from a regional expert in the field. Although defense attorneys argued that such testimony would make the defendant's actions more "reasonable" since in fact there are many practical alternatives to nuclear energy, the judge could not comprehend the link. This effort marked the end of the defense's case.

In summation the prosecutor argued the consequences of an acquittal stating that such a verdict would be an open invitation for nuclear opponents to occupy Comanche Peak in the future. "You will be granting these people a license to come back to this county and break the law," he said, holding up photos of the seven male defendants whose hair was longest, beards thickest and dress most unconventional. "Just because they think nuclear power is wrong is no excuse for these people to break any law they want."

The defense attorneys first reviewed the law that gave the jury the right to vote for acquittal. If they found the threats from Comanche Peak more significant than the harm caused by the occupation and/or they felt the defendants acted out of duress because of those threats, they would have to vote "not guilty." Even though the 48 broke the law by climbing the fence, their acts of trespassing could be excused for these reasons. The attorneys then reviewed the political context of the trial, arguing that the prosecutor's narrow legalistic viewpoint did not encompass the full meaning of what occurred in the courtroom these last three days. "If he had been the State's attorney in Massachusetts, then he (the prosecutor) would have prosecuted the patriots of the Boston Tea Party," said one. They ended their presentations with a quote from Einstein: "To the village square we must carry the facts of atomic energy... from there must come America's voice."

The jury received the case at 5:15 p.m. Friday and retired to the "deliberating room" as the judge called it. The media and some of the more cynical spectators believed they would not be long in returning a guilty verdict; despite Sternglasss' and Bertells' testimony, they could not believe a Glen Rose jury would have *trouble convicting the defendants of trespassing. The 48 would be lucky to get off with a small fine.*

But as the first thirty minutes passed then an hour, it became clear that something different was going to happen. Hour after hour passed, then a break for dinner then another long period of waiting. At 11:15 p.m. the jury sent a note to the judge stating that they were "hopelessly deadlocked" after nearly five hours of deliberations. The judge brought them back to the courtroom and upon confirming the deadlock, dismissed them and declared a mistrial. Word spread that the jury had been split four to two in favor of acquittal. (The two jurors who voted for conviction have close relatives working at the plant and people who have talked with them speculate this might have been a factor in their decision. One of the two stated he is concerned about nuclear power after

hearing testimony at the trial.)

Jubilation crept slowly across the benches where 20 to 30 defendants sat through the entire trial, then pandemonium as their weariness faded and the reality of the jury's action sank in.

Outside the courtroom the peanut farmer and the part time hog farmer, both of whom had voted for acquittal, spoke to the defendants and media. "At first I thought it was a plain trespassing case, but I learned differently," said one, brushing back tears and shaking occupiers' hands. "If I knew then what I know now I might have climbed that fence too," added the other. Both said their minds had been changed considerably about the plant and they would talk to friends and neighbors about what they had learned. Asked what advice he would give to the people in the area about Comanche Peak, the peanut farmer said he would tell them to take a "good hard look "at the plant. Even the prosecutor, who kept whatever opinions he had about nuclear power to himself, stated that the occupants might be "doing the county a favor."

In retrospect it is still remarkable. Four out of six Glen Rose residents stated in effect that trespassing to stop Comanche Peak was justified, considering the harm the plant would be to the community once online. Four people who no one would have pegged as sympathetic to lawbreakers or anti-nuke protesters.

Perhaps their action cannot be fully appreciated

by those who have never lived in a small "company" town or who are not familiar with the political and cultural context in which the four arrived at their decision.

The trial was also able to put the issues of nuclear power on display as never before, both in Dallas and Fort Worth papers and, in the courtroom, filled with citizen spectators. The media went into detail in reporting Sternglasss' and Bertells' testimony about the cancer hazards of nukes, issues that would not have been covered at a rally or a regulatory hearing. It was an effective teach-in on radiation harms for North Texas as could have been taught by the activists themselves.

This trial was an exception to the rule, as most attempts to get evidence on nuclear power introduced in occupation trials are denied by the judge. Nevertheless, if occupiers can successfully put nukes on trial, they have a unique and excellent opportunity to organize at the local level.

—End of remarks by Jim Schermbeck—

After the mistrial was announced, Life Force members and our supporters burst into the town square and spilled into the parking lot, singing and shouting "No Nukes around here." The local people had agreed about the problems of the plant, yet they couldn't grasp the joy and true disbelief that the efforts and energy spent to get our case before the people had truly paid off. For a short time afterwards, I felt that justice could prevail, yet this was too easy, and the people may not be listening.

If anyone was paying attention, it was the legal system in Somervell County and the atomic industry via Texas Electric Service Company. By mid-October 1979, the Somervell County Commissioners had authorized Charles Jordan, county attorney, to hire a special prosecutor to help him in the retrial of the forty-eight criminal trespass cases that burdened the county court docket. In 1979, the Texas State Bar had only two members in Somervell County, Judge Sam Freas and County Attorney Charles Jordan. More information can be found in the transcripts of the trial in Glen Rose Texas, June 27-29, 1979. Also, the December 14, 1979 issue of The Texas Observer has an excellent article covering the trials.

Preparations for the new trials were also being made by the defendants. Noting

the state had decided to try the 48 defendants one at a time, we met and signed our names in the order in which we felt the need to state our case. First was Mavis Belisle and second, Sister Patricia Ridgley (both later found guilty), and so forth down the line to me, counting in at number 48.

With all the vigor of the cartoon character Atom Ant, the special prosecutor, Johnson County Judge Tommy Altaras, waded into the trials. In the realm of people-versus-profits, the defendant in the person of Mavis Belisle, one of the organizers of the Comanche Peak Life Force, was the first to be on trial. We stood along, beside and with Mavis as she bravely faced the upcoming whirlwind. Her trial was set for the end of November 1979.

With the dedication of another cartoon character, Wile E. Coyote, (who never gave up) the CPLF began planning the second occupation of the Comanche Peak nuclear plant. Meetings were held all summer concentrating on how to support Mavis, and how to begin with another action which would be a direct step to a nuclear-free Texas. It was hoped that more protesters would join our ranks.

CHAPTER V

Occupation November 25, 1979 and the Yellow School Bus

Nuke hunting in general was particularly good in the fall of 1979. Volunteers all over the world were taking to the fields, woods, rivers and the streets to help stop the construction of nuclear power plants. On September 29, the Shad Alliance targeted the Shoreham nuclear power plant on Long Island and then

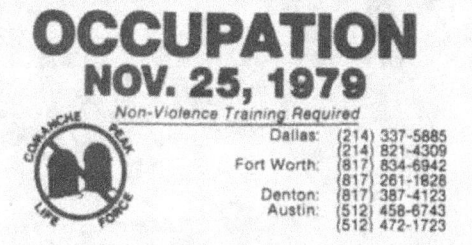

on October 6, 1979 east coast volunteers and others from around the country, including members of the Yellow Rose Life Force, attempted to stop construction of the Seabrook nuclear station in New Hampshire. While they did not meet

their goal, the hardy souls showed the world that a lot of Americans were opposed to the nuclear industry and were willing to act in order to stop it, regardless of the risks.

I guess more than anything the attitude of the folks returning for Seabrook caused me to realize the urgent

need to stop Comanche Peak while it was still being built. The people living around Seabrook had voted twice to stop the construction, yet the Nuclear Regulatory Commission refused to stop a construction permit for the Public Service Company of New Hampshire. Over the course of three years, nearby towns voted against nuclear power as well. It became clear that the will of the people of the seacoast towns of

New Hampshire have been ignored. This made me feel there would be no justice in Texas, and that we were on our own. A nuclear-free state is one of the goals of the anti-nuclear movement worldwide. Austria is a nuclear free zone, as is Vancouver, Canada.

It was the consensus of the affinity groups that another occupation/action would keep public attention on issues at Comanche Peak such as cost overruns and the lack of plans for dealing with the nuclear waste produced after the plant went online. It was important to take advantage of the mistrial and the public support gathering around the first action. The spokesperson for each affinity group within the Life Force gathered in Waco, Texas on October 20, to plan for the coming action planned for November 25, 1979.

Over a period of four to five hours, using the consensus decision-making process, about a dozen ideas or proposals were agreed upon. Among these was the decision to use the original guidelines in the CPLF handbook. All guidelines would go into effect when the first person arrived in staging area and be followed until the last person was released from jail. Red t-shirts and black armbands were to be worn by Life Force members, with other t-shirts would be available for sale to the public. A baseline health study was discussed and a need to check among locals for support was also agreed upon. Also to be considered was the recently passed law in Texas (Senate Bill 952) that sharply increased penalties for trespassing on utility company property, including the up to six-month jail sentence and fines up to $1,000. Lewis Pitts consulted with legal experts in Austin and found the law did not apply to power plants until they were in operation. The days seemed numbered for non-violent direct action in Texas.

The spokes meetings were a gathering of one representative from each affinity group now numbering about a dozen, deciding on a facilitator, writing an agenda and discussing each item. The following week another meeting was scheduled to be held in White Hawk Valley, north of Denton and the last spoke meeting before the occupation was set for November 11 in Glen Rose to tie up loose ends and also to distribute leaflets to folks in Glen Rose on why another action of civil disobedience was needed. Several proposals were sent back to the affinity groups via the spokes (representatives). These ranged from the intention of staying three days on site, to each affinity group drawing up a rough draft for an on-site (nuclear plant property) statement.  Ideas ranged from a demand for the shutdown of Comanche Peak and recognizing that we are all Texans, and our intention was not to hassle workers. The lack of viable legal recourse was discussed, as was the need to recognize the true foe: the military-industrial complex via Texas Utilities. All were deemed to be particularly important.

Ideas for a budget were discussed at the spokes meeting, consisting of three parts: preparation, occupation and post-occupation cost, with each affinity group paying a base figure, depending on the need of CPLF and then a percentage of amounts raised over and above that figure was later accepted and used by affinity groups for several months afterward. All affinity groups proved to be very capable of raising funds when needed. The building of trust that began early in the non-violence training classes strengthened as time and planning continued, which played an important role throughout the existence of the CPLF.

The national media spread the news of the actions at Shoreham and Seabrook, giving courage to CPLF members for the upcoming trials. The number of people involved in the struggle against nuclear power began to grow, yet there was no real groundswell of support for simply climbing the fence and getting a ticket from the sheriff's office. The true support seemed to be in favor of stopping the nuclear power plant by more legal means or becoming more radical and direct in the area of civil disobedience. Because of this, anyone proposing violence was quickly denounced and sometimes called out as an undercover agent. Students of history understand that Texan revolutionists have an interesting and explosive history.

With the increased number of people, the Dallas affinity group now contained nearly thirty souls. This is too many people for the consensus decision-making process that was the foundation of the affinity groups. Meetings commonly lasting a couple of hours could go on indefinitely with thirty people. A natural split was around the corner, so another affinity group was formed. According to where you lived, the Dallas or the Garland affinity group was your place to participate. That was one way to form an affinity group, but not necessarily the best way. Living in Eastvale, a small community east of Lake Lewisville north of Dallas, Carobeth and I joined the Garland group. An improvement was made later, by forming due to true affinity rather than distance traveled. In time however a new group, Rainbow affinity group, was to play several roles in the future actions of Comanche Peak Life Force and its allies.

Statewide, the numbers of anti-nuke activists had grown to several hundred, perhaps more, Texans had organized with high and hopeful spirits. We felt the need to speak and act against nuclear power was both necessary and incredibly important. The number of affinity groups within the CPLF numbered between 15 and 20. The groups, through spokes meetings, regular affinity group meetings, and using consensus, readied for the announced Second Occupation of the Comanche Peak Steam Electric (nuclear powered) Plant on November 25, 1979. Thousands of red leaflets were printed, divided and posted as a statewide call to the action.

Gathering at White Hawk Valley near Denton, Texas on October 27, the spokespersons first toured the site then settled under an uncompleted ferro-cement dome. Thus began the task of working out the logistics for the November 25 action. The list of things to discuss included cooperation-versus non-cooperation with the authorities, the Lone Star Alliance (a loose knit group opposing nuclear energy in Texas), self-security, neutral observers, trials, denied asset of plant property, and the likelihood of a children's action at the front gate of the main road.

Cooperation-versus-noncooperation with the authorities was the idea discussed the most. To push the struggle to a more militant nonviolent course of action, noncooperation was the way to make a stronger statement for individuals or groups. Many felt this was needed for simple symbolic action wasn't working, and a more deliberate stand was in order. Even though tickets or citations were written, we later discovered they were dismissed to avoid a public forum via the trials of those arrested. A letter to every registered voter in Somervell County with information regarding the problems with nuclear power plants and the expected dangers if Comanche Peak can operate was approved at the White Valley meeting. The printing and mailing was carried out by the Agape affinity group in Austin. Later, during Mavis's trial, the mailing was ruled by Judge Freas a contempt of court as possibly influencing future jurors, and CPLF was ordered not to repeat this action while ongoing trials continued.

While preparations within the Garland affinity group began, we hoped for at least one day or more on site. Our lightweight alternative energy display was to be cardboard covered with aluminum foil in a concave shape used as a model for a solar cooker. Other plans were to start a native plant identification class, look at having a windmill set up and have first aid, water and plenty of food on hand or close

by. Also needed were tents, sleeping bags, wool blankets and other goods. In case of denied access by security, our group came up with several ideas, including having affinity groups splitting up and trying different means of entry or returning the next day in smaller more mobile affinity groups.

In the area of bail solidarity, if those arrested decided not to show personal identification as a statement of noncooperation, we would push for their release to personal recognizance or maybe a small bond though our legal team. The cutoff date suggested for a new affinity group to act in the occupation was November 21.

An important part of the preparation for the action was the greasing of the law enforcement community. Lewis Pitts was tireless in his efforts with the CPLF, doing the legal leg work and always positive about our efforts. The Somervell County Sheriff's office and the officials at the nuclear electric station were informed of the nature and purpose of the upcoming protest. Legal advisors and organizers of the Life Force were led to believe that the authorities would allow protestors to cross the fence and demonstrate the alternative energy displays. The different affinity groups were ready to use these as symbols of determination showing a non-nuclear energy Texas could be a reality. These included several small windmills, solar panels with batteries, a magnifying glass wood burning display and several solar cooking devices. Yet a sense of uneasiness grew as the final stage was set for the gathering of several hundred Texans and friends for the action on November 25, 1979, it was as if Murphy's law was about to be explained to

those not familiar with its meaning.

The beginning of the occupation began on Saturday morning, November 24, 1979. The staging area was set up at the rustic stockade on the banks of the Paluxy River, about three or four blocks south of downtown Glen Rose. By midday most had arrived and began to set up shelters for the cool night approaching. A general feeling of oneness and community spread throughout the gathering in a way that made instant friends of total strangers and laid the foundation for some friendships that would truly stand the test of time. Reunions were held by those who had returned from Seabrook. Despite the feeling of community, we noticed a few stares and curious eyes watching some of us. There was one fellow with bulky video equipment who seemed to sweep the area with the grace of a hawk watching chickens gathering in a field. It began to make a few of us paranoid until we learned this was a camera crew from Europe making a documentary

on the American anti-nuclear power movement.

Not to be caught off guard, peacekeepers in pairs patrolled the outskirts of the area in revolving shifts of two or three hours each. As a seemingly peaceful night approached word came to our affinity group that one of Austin's, and possibly Houston's, groups had become alarmed at the fact that some affinity groups were not going to cooperate with authorities when arrested. A spokes meeting was quickly called, fears were put to rest and hurt feelings were bandaged with all the diplomacy of true Texas politics. Out of this discussion came the first crack of what in time eventually would erode into a split. Some of us supported more direct action and others wished only to play politics with marches, rallies and petition drives.

The residents of Glen Rose surely took notice when our group began singing anti-nuke anthems and chanted

"No Nukes!" Before sunset Saturday, the sound of a media helicopter churned the nippy air. Making sure we were noticed, the words NO NUKES were spelled out on the ground with our bodies linked together forming the letters. Quick decision-making paid off with the group, as it soon

would many times over. After this brief, but lively encounter, the members of the CPLF joined hands, forming a human circle to sing a chorus of The Cow Song and finished with Woody Guthrie's iconic *This Land Is My Land*.

Night turned into day and the smell of oatmeal, fruit and coffee mixed with the sounds of awakening activists on their way to the future, one step at a time. Black armbands were passed around as groups gathered to ready their supplies for what was planned to be a long action.

Those who felt the need gathered and began a small religious service, with local clergy leading them in prayer. The anarchists among us painted on bare chests and faces and romped around loudly, disrupting the entire camp. A free spirited young woman named Heidi cheerfully paraded around bare-chested, with the words "Yellow Rose" colorfully painted across her breasts. The modest minded in the group were taken by surprise, while the more open-minded of the bunch laughed and respected Heidi for being so free in her expression. She was presented with a red t-shirt, which quieted the roar and allowed thoughts to focus on the goal at hand: to occupy Comanche Peak. This little episode played out quickly, but I enjoyed the spontaneous nature of the moment, also since I had a camera to document the moment.

The religious and the playful, coming together for a common cause, an action against what both held to be a bad thing, the Comanche Peak nuclear plant.

The time set for the action was 10:00 a.m. on Sunday, November 25, 1979. By 9:30 we started to gather in and around the cars, trucks, and vans that would transport the entire group to the front gates of the nuclear plant. The ride to the parking area didn't last long, and before I knew it we had formed a huge line of about 250 people. To our surprise, there were dozens of supporters and curious onlookers already gathered around the locked gates, with people on both sides of the fence and road leading into the plant site. Also in sight were a dozen utility employees and officials, along with several yellow school buses provided by Texas Utilities to haul the protestors after our arrest. This didn't look like the ideal entry point for the prolonged action for which we had prepared.

Armed with ladders, flags, backpacks and alternative energy displays, we approach the gates. Moving to the right of the gate, off the road and onto a grassy knoll, the stiles or ladders were placed in position.

As I recall, Sheriff Frank Laramore spoke sternly into the bullhorn, saying "Stop there, if you cross the fence you are trespassing and will be arrested." The next few minutes truly showed me what confusion due to high emotions could do. The plan, while discussed, wasn't practical, and quick decision-making was needed. Access had not been defined and the trust put into the negotiations had been betrayed.

Over the roar and chants of those further back in line, it seemed like those crossing the fence were being placed under arrest as soon as an officer could reach them. That was totally different from the agreement with our legal aid and the Sheriff's department to allow us to set up energy displays. A group of folks from Yellow Rose formed a circle and linked arms before peacefully being led one by one to the waiting buses. The first bus filled almost instantly so I, along with a group of twenty or so others, were directed to the second bus. The remaining protesters, who were arrested, were put into Department of Public Safety vehicles and driven to jail. In all, 103 people willingly crossed the fence and were arrested on that day.

I was on the bus with more than twenty truly angry people who felt they had been betrayed. Jim Shermbeck, one of the original organizers of the CPLF, boarded the bus when it was nearly full. "Anything goes, they lied to us," he shouted. Yes, "exactly," was my first thought. At the same time, a quick decision was made, as a spokesman was decided on and discussion began about what to do since we were off-site and being driven to jail. It was suggested that we stay on the bus instead of turning

ourselves over to the authorities. The bus belonged to Texas Electric. It was decided that those who wished to leave could, and those who wanted to stay would occupy the bus. When

the first bus arrived at the Glen Rose jail, all the passengers cooperated and went inside where they were written tickets for criminal trespassing. Not knowing of the second bus rebellion, it came as a shock to the authorities, press and fellow protesters alike that such an action was taking place. After all, other protesters were given citations and released on personal recognizance. A spokes meeting was quickly held in the parking area by the jail. The different affinity groups decidedly supported our splinter group remaining on the bus, with some reservations. No one aboard the second bus had opted to leave and the newly christened "Rosa Parks" affinity group was formed.

Those of us on the bus and supporters outside settled in for a long wait. Discussion inside the bus ranged from wanting to return to the plant site, to those who simply enjoyed what was going on, 'the happening.' Face-painting, singing of a new song "We all live on a Yellow School Bus," soul searching and

picture taking lasted for several hours. Bonds were quickly built as several locals light heartily tried to empty the bus by placing a snake through one of the windows, since the example of seeing a snake and taking action was used as the defense of the 48 defendants as "duress and necessity." This effort failed as supporters surrounded the bus to prevent a repeat attempt. Talks continued between authorities, legal aid and those on the bus.

It wasn't clear if the Texas Department of Safety decided to empty the bus due to their own anger or due to orders given. No matter the case, two DPS officers came on the bus and asked us to leave. When we refused, they picked the first person in their reach, which was me. Having decided not to cooperate with the officers, I was carried

gingerly with one officer holding my feet and the other my shoulders as we exited the bus via the front door. After being placed on the Sheriff's floor, I showed my identification, was written a ticket and shown out the door.

As I exited the Sheriff's office, I was met with hugs and high fives from the supporters outside. I honestly felt there was only one thing to do, and that was to return to my comrades on the bus. I did just that by climbing through an open window on the backside of the bus, to the cheers and approval from fellow occupiers. Because the DPS was not willing to remove each person forcefully, they did not enter the bus again until the stand-off ended late that afternoon.

After five hours on the bus, we decided the point was made and voluntarily departed the bus. All aboard received a citation for criminal trespassing. The Life Force returned to T's place to regroup, eat supper and grab a beer. In the end, I wasn't given a second ticket—the trespass was at the plant, not on the bus.

With emotions and spirits high, we circled to talk about the day. We discussed the final part of Mavis's trial which was going to take place the next day. Many people involved in the action left Glen Rose, yet there were plenty of people left to carry on a party, for this day ended the approach of symbolic actions against Comanche Peak Nuclear Station. Those camped in Glen Rose awoke to the chill of late November, and the fact that one of our numbers was on trial and may well be found guilty.

The jury found Mavis guilty, and the judge sentenced her to pay the maximum fine of $200. The trial of Mavis Belisle

and that of Sister Patricia Ridgeley were modern versions of frontier justice at best. Mavis was described as a "middle-aged hippie" by the special prosecutor Tommy Altaras (Atom

Ant). "They got their best foot forward" he later said. "Out of the 48 people, Ms. Belisle was the best defendant. She doesn't look like the rest of them, she doesn't talk like the rest of them. She doesn't smell like them. She's clean." Earlier in his closing argument he admonished the jurors not to be "fooled by a middle-aged hippie who hasn't found another cause to fight." Quick decisions by the judge and the second occupation on November 25 sealed her faith. The slogan "people before profits" came to mind. There are those who profit from the government subsidies for nuclear power and

there are those of us who are truly afraid of relying on such a deadly energy source.

Mavis refused to pay her fine to keep it in the public eye, so Judge Freas sentenced her to fifty-five days for her part in the June 10 action, as well as her role in putting nuclear power on trial in Texas. Those of us who gathered outside the Glen Rose courthouse were faced with problems which became evident at Mavis's trial. The first was what to do about the trials of the forty-seven remaining defendants. Sister Patricia was to be tried next. Her trial was well attended by supporters such as the Sisters of Saint Mary from Houston, Dallas and Fort Worth instead of the flower children-type protesters. Judge Freas ruled defense witnesses, a public health official from Colorado and a former quality assurance inspector for Texas Utilities, could testify. Yet the jurors weren't allowed to listen to the damming information of shoddy construction practices and questionable inspection procedures. Sister Patricia was also found guilty, but thankfully she wasn't victim of the name-calling from Atom Ant.

Our next problem came to light as we circled to embrace our thoughts and feelings. Each person spoke freely for a moment, and the group as began to feel stronger for it. One supporter among us, River, was a self-proclaimed "Rainbower." He entered the circle speaking of Mother Earth and Father Sky, touching the four corners with his eagle feather. A photographer edged closer to take a picture of this unique fellow, River sprung on him as if his life had been threatened. It was clear to all that the photographer meant River no harm. In restraining River, we saw that no longer was this a group moment but a very public display. Also, we were reminded that trust is a fragile thing which can be quickly lost.

CHAPTER VI
Winter 1979 to March 28, 1980 and the Road Gang

As reactions from the November 25 occupation and trials began to surface, many found the bus episode silly while others found it a springboard to future events. As the later idea spread and gained more support, more direct action was openly discussed and acted upon.

Meetings and strategy sessions were the order of the day through most of the winter months. Brave souls began hiking, wandering and exploring the boundaries of the thousands of acres around the Comanche Peak plant. Those scouting trips were to prove invaluable for future actions.

The winter spokes meetings produced written goals and the strategy of the CPLF which were taken back for all members to review and ponder. The goals were as follows: to stop Comanche Peak and all nuclear power; to rid the world of nuclear weapons (this was always a given with the group); and to actively support the national actions at weapons facilities and plants such as Pantex in North Texas

or Rocky Flats in Colorado. The penalty for trespassing on and/or damaging a government missile silo is a felony and carried a long prison sentence. The strategy of CPLF was non-violent resistance and self-awareness to accomplish these goals. Also, to actively promoting life sustaining social, economic and political alternatives. Truth be told, it was a large task for such a small number of people, but it was winter (a time for planning) and we were meeting in Austin (home of the small University of Texas reactor, a 31.3 MW TGRIA Mark II nuclear reactor built on campus in the late 1950's for research.) The Austin area was also home of the Yellow Rose affinity group, which encompassed eco-anarchism via consensus decision making. Yellow Rose always gave a lot more positive energy than can be put down in words.

Another thought about the protest came up for discussion: why continue go to the nuclear plant and protest? Why not just lobby and let the system stop the plant? It was argued that this approach had already been tried without much success. The response from the militant members (and more logical for me and the rest of our tight knit group from East Dallas and Garland) was why not go to the nuke? It was the belly of the nuclear beast and we needed to continue the struggle.

Several affinity groups began to cluster and discuss a direct action, for the Dallas-Garland group the target was easy and to get volunteers was even easier. Many brave souls from Austin, Fort Worth (after a little convincing), and the Dallas-Garland group were more than willing to step up. There were also brave souls from Oklahoma who were ready for a more militant action, something more than fence jumping.

But before wading into those waters, it should be noted that around late 1979 and early 1980 there were some changes in the organization. Several of our organizers and trainers left, including Debra Sachas and Dick Lee, who inspired actions and lit many a radical flame in North Texas. Debra and

Dick helped create a timeline to build a united front against Comanche Peak, and they encouraged us to be direct and active until the injustice was righted. Some passages in the CPLF handbooks were written with their help.

Hell, what could be more direct and take more action than to barricade the entrance to the plant? That was what we needed at Comanche Peak and Texas Utilities and the time to do it was the morning of March 28, 1980—the one-year

[Newspaper clipping headline: "Capitol rally draws 600 nuclear opponents"]

anniversary of the disaster at the Three Mile Island nuclear power plant in Pennsylvania. For the few of us who were planning the action, the goal was to prepare, then remain as silent about it as possible. A "Citizens March for Safe Energy" was scheduled at the same time in Austin. Protests at two locations would make for great press coverage.

The Dallas-Garland affinity group consisted of fifteen to twenty people. Of those in the group, eight to ten of us had become close friends. Trust had been built among the group not just with their words, but from their actions. This trust helped grow bonds of friendship and solidarity which would grow stronger, be tested over time, yet still be cherished years later.

Our resources to conduct a barricade of the main entrance of Comanche Peak were growing daily as we gathered materials in the Dallas area. A growing stockpile of tires, rope, barrels, broken pieces of sidewalk concrete and other materials helped motivate us to seek volunteers from the other affinity groups within the CPLF. Since independent actions by small groups were still new territory, a recruiting

drive drew favor with the Yellow Rose Life Force in Austin and some volunteers from Fort Worth.

Only two planning meetings took place between the first of March and the morning of March 28. The first took place on Palo Pinto Street in Dallas, an older duplex rented by two active members of CPLF. One side was rented by a

straightforward young lady, who worked for a large airline, and the other side by a single dad working as a freelance carpenter. Road trips to Glen Rose served as brainstorming sessions so long meetings weren't needed.

Basic information such as the width of the road, the number of guards that would be on duty, and the flow of traffic on the Highway 201 (now Highway 56) intersection of United Way (the road leading to the Plant now known as Comanche Lane) was reported. At the time, there was no ten-foot cyclone fence around the property and little traffic, except when workers were changing shifts and an occasional supply truck coming or going. It should be noted that the plant was out of sight of the western entrance, perhaps a mile or two to the east, next to Squaw Creek Lake. Findings from earlier outings to learn more about the area around the plant began to show their value. The guardhouse sat about half a mile east of United Way Drive entrance from Highway 201, at this time the outside security fence was being worked on and their excess fencing came in handy during dawn hours of the 28th.

The most productive reconnaissance mission also happened in the first week of March when two members of the Comanche Peak Life Force entered Texas Utilities property via the front gate on none other than a tour bus. A friend in

the Life Force was employed at an engineering firm that did some work for Texas Utilities. A tour of Comanche Peak was offered to the firm and this is how we were able to see the construction of the nuke up close. On the bus with about thirty professional engineers and invited guests (yours truly). There was no security check, but we had drinks and snacks. We were driven around the property and shown the sights, including a billboard in the shadow of the still uncompleted

domes which showed a rendering of a working nuclear steam reactor. We also saw the containment buildings and were driven to a plateau on a small mountain of soil east of the nuke, which was a place that would be significant in future protests. It was there that we exited the bus as Texas Utilities officials offered us sodas with a side of lies. The time spent on the bus tour and taking snapshots of the surrounding terrain and buildings proved to be valuable in planning future actions. While I was taking photos of the terrain there were several curious looks from the engineers. On the return ride to Dallas, the engineers seemed more puzzled than ever on the need for nuclear power. They posed pointed questions to a TU official, who had answers that simply didn't stand up to the facts. They asked what was to be done with the waste, as well as where and how long it would be stored. The answer given was that the final site had not been chosen, causing more concerned looks from the engineers.

Trips to and around the main entrance on United Way always paid off, recording worker arrivals and departures, checking visibility at night. These general scouting activities were carried out by three or four people, sometimes in a group or at least in pairs. One of our members, Albert Most, worked as a laborer for Brown and Root, the company contracted to build Comanche Peak. In that role, he was able to gain knowledge of the outlying service roads and worker schedules.

With each trip to Glen Rose, the stash of materials to be used in the action grew. Several 55-gallon drums, old discarded tires, and lumber were stored nearby. The larger items were placed under a small culvert literally across the road from the gates.

Less than a hundred yards south of the main road leading to the nuke, a local couple were selling small overgrown cedar and mesquite filled lots of land. A few of us put up a hundred dollars each and made a down payment on one small plot. This deal was made with a handshake and $500.00, but it was never completed for papers weren't drawn up and signed. Despite that detail, we used the plot of land and the surrounding area to store materials, rest after scouting runs and to park cars, which could not be seen from the highway. Workers from the plant lived in nearby trailers, houses and neatly constructed shelters. These folks were friendly, many would approach us and strike up a conversation, inviting us into their homes and telling about their plans. They never really asked us about why we were there, but it wasn't long before the cat was let out of the bag, so to speak. The local press corps was soon poking around, with reports such as "Protesters buy next to the nuclear plant, what is their intent?" Locals were shocked, as they had no idea who we were or what our purpose was. Soon they were saying that perhaps we should return to Dallas and quit coming to Glen Rose to start trouble. Although they were good people, the locals didn't seem to have a layman's knowledge of nuclear power. They just knew that jobs at Comanche Peak were paying their bills and good jobs were hard to find.

After all the press about us, the couple who were selling us the land stopped the sale and kept our $500 "good faith" deposit. Without a receipt or anything to legally show we had

Connie Johnson says she did not know protesters were buying the land.

paid them, we gave up the lot. However, it was money well spent as we got good use of it. Besides, the date of the action was near.

The second meeting for this action occurred in Austin and took less time than it normally took to just do introductions at the larger CPLF meetings.

After a group hug and smoke, the scenario for the action was briefly discussed. The folks from Yellow Rose seemed ready for whatever the rest of us had planned; "just tell us what time to be there," was their reply to the information. The shared feeling of action speaks louder than words prevailed. Without the dogma of politics, a real trust had been built over the past year that enabled planning, tactics, and actions to develop freely. This group of Earth-centered anarchists shared their love and willingness to clash with authority whenever the opportunity came about, even at the risk of personal sacrifice. This attitude was something I had read about but seldom seen acted upon. These were folks like me, people who valued independence but who were ready to tear down the walls erected by past cultural norms.

Photos taken earlier at the nuke were passed around for amusement, since the action was to be at the main gate out of sight of the nuke. Ideas for more barricade materials were talked about, and folks were encouraged to bring all the materials and volunteers possible. To meet at the trailer in town Thursday night to get ready for the hit the next day was the plan. Everyone was in good cheer after a group hug and some partying. We were prepared from some real direct action. We were to stay within non-violence guidelines, there would be no leaflets or handbooks. The press was notified on March 27 about the action at Comanche Peak the next day. Combined with the anniversary of the disaster at Three Mile Island, along with "Citizens For Safe Energy March" to be held in Austin, we felt assured of media coverage plus having our cameras on hand to record the event as well.

Secrecy wasn't at a paranoid level, but concern was taken since we were trying to stop or at least slow the construction of the plant. When driving sixty to seventy miles one-way to hide materials there was always a sense of awe at the sight of Comanche Peak, the plateau and Comanche Peak Steam Electric Station only meters apart, looming in the distance as we approached Glen Rose from the east. The days before March 28 had been used to move everything within reason as close to the main entrance on United Way Drive without being spotted by the guards at the checkpoint two hundred yards away. Old car tires were either dumped along the side of the road directly across from the four-lane wide entrance way, which was divided only by a large barrel of sand with a sign atop stating private road. More blockade materials were placed under the culvert bridge. Also stashed were short pieces of cyclone fence that had been gathered during raids along the fence lines which would soon surround the main areas of the plant, if not the total 4,000 acres. Some lumber, chains, an old washing machine and more 55-gallon barrels were stored at the plot of land we had tried to purchase. Feeling swindled out of the real estate sale but comforted by the fact the lot was particularly useful in this action of frontier justice.

Waking up Friday, March 28th to a gentle rain and a cool breeze, we gained strength as the final part of what was the strongest action anti-nuclear foes in the South had taken to date unfolded. Meeting at the lot, we busied ourselves gathering materials and waiting for one last truckload carrying barrels painted yellow with radioactive signs and partly filled with rocks and broken pieces of Dallas sidewalks to arrive.

From the scouting we knew within a few minutes of what time the first shift of workers would arrive. In the darkness prior to a Texas sunrise, we left the small encampment area in a hurry and headed to the front gates. The gates were newly erected frames made of tube steel with no cyclone fencing attached. We rolled out the barrels which had been placed in the back seats of compact cars and in the bed of Carobeths' blue Datsun King Cab pickup truck. Placing the barrels and washing machine in the middle of United Way Drive along with several wooden sawhorse barriers, we also scattered the broken pieces of Dallas sidewalks across the road for good measure and chained the gates shut. The blockade began.

In less than ten minutes we had closed the entrance to the Comanche Peak Nuke. This act of resistance brought emotions like those felt by the patriots who threw boxes of tea into a harbor or to those who blocked an entrance of a draft board office to help stop an unjust war. Within seconds headlights from the first workers of the next shift began to appear as daylight broke over the central Texas Hill Country. Workers in pickups began to stop one after another at the entrance asking, "what the hell is going on?" They were met with assuring smiles and told the plant was being closed and they could take the day off. Comments of "these are the protesters we have heard about" or "I'm going to be late" were heard. Previous actions had not involved the actual slowdown or stoppage of access to the plant. Those actions had been symbolic and greased to the point TU officials and the Sheriff knew pretty much what, when and how the protest would occur. The face to face interaction with the workers was new for our group but was a good opportunity for explaining our reason for closing the road. Conversation with the workers was positive until the realization that they were going to be late for work. Some finally turned their trucks around and left. But others took a more proactive approach and rolled the brightly painted barrels out of the road and took bolt cutters to the chain wrapped around the skeleton front gates.

The workers rolled east on United Way grinding the gears of their Ford F-150s and Chevy Silverados trying to beat the clock so they could punch in to work on time. A quick decision was made to retreat to our staging area and regroup as the first wave of workers went by. There were mixed emotions since we had stopped the flow of traffic for about fifteen minutes but not sure what to do next. The sun was still rising in the Texas sky when Elna Christopher, the embedded reporter from the Dallas Morning News, arrived. She was a go-get-it-done woman, who had always reported fairly on our behalf. Elna had been given the location of our staging area since it was no longer a secret that the protestors were trying to buy some land in the area.

She, along with photographer David Woo, arrived and promptly asked "Well, where is the blockade?" Without much more than a few glances and nods we headed back to the entrance. Our consensus training continued to pay off. The hideout was only a hundred yards at best from the gates. Within a few minutes we were again standing in front of our destiny.

The night crew had left, and the first wave of day workers got in after our brief encounter. Having used most, but not all, of the materials in what would come to be known as the first wave of the barricade/blockade by the Comanche Peak Road Gang. Taking advantage of the lull in worker traffic, the rest of the tires and fencing were laid out, the gates were

closed and locked using a pair of ten-dollar handcuffs I bought at an East Dallas police supply store. Our main scout, Kent Wilson, climbed atop the gates and hung a banner the folks from Austin had made. On it was a beautifully drawn scene of a woman sitting with knees bent and her head bowed with the Three Mile Island nuke in the background, with the words, No More Three Mile Island written in red. With the embedded news team taking pictures (which are classic in my mind), we readied to form a human blockade to stop the second flow of workers scheduled to arrive forty-five minutes to an hour after the first wave of workers. It seemed the longest time before they began to appear, perhaps word of this protest was slowly spreading via home phones, citizen band radios or walkie talkies.

The second wave of workers weren't as cheerful as the previous ones and tried to kick the gate open. They nearly succeeded, but the handcuffs held. That was the sign we needed to enforce our grit and determination. Sheriff Laramore soon arrived on the scene as expected followed by the yellow school bus. The mood was calm as the ten members of the Road Gang were arrested. Several of the women decided not to cooperate and had to be carried onto the bus. The support crew followed us back to Glen Rose, where our resolve grew even stronger. The spirit on the bus going to Glen Rose was loving, yet strong and determined. It was a great feeling—hard to describe but it will always be remembered. This quick homegrown action brought a sense of euphoria and zeal to all the activists statewide. The press coverage helped to spread the word of our action like a prairie fire throughout Texas and the entire country.

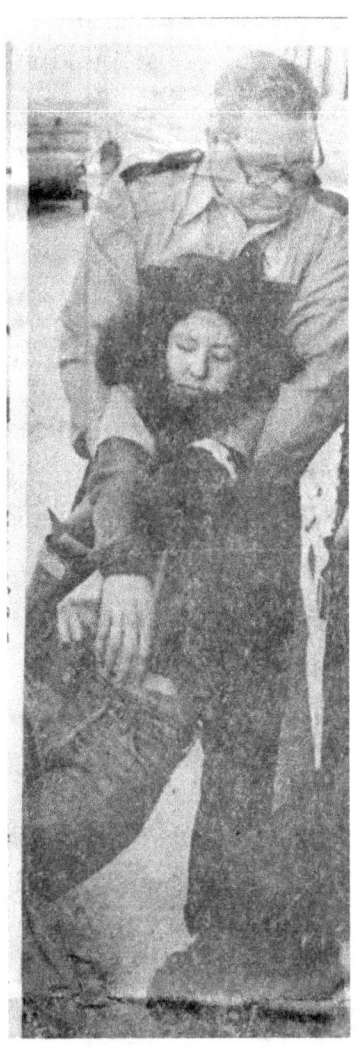

Six women and four men comprised this newly formed affinity group the Road Gang. We had come together from Oklahoma, Dallas, and Fort Worth, and we were joined by a few free-spirited revolutionary souls from Austin. Participating in simple, yet edgy, actions like the barricade at Comanche Peak, can help form bonds which last a lifetime. This was one of the building blocks for nonviolent civil disobedience actions in the decades that followed.

I was arrested, along with the three other men and the six women, and bused to Glen Rose then to Granbury. We had all previously decided not to set bail or pay a fine. Settling, instead, to spend several days at the Hood County jail. The men were placed into one cell and the six women were divided into two separate cells. The women were denied fresh water and basic privacy, which only seemed to toughen their resolve. Old West chivalry was lost on the Hood County Sheriff, who wasn't ready to have women prisoners for any length of time. While most of the women were prepared for what lay ahead, one of the women was a bit confused about the fact that acts of civil disobedience should not be taken lightly. She joined our action after sitting in on one nonviolent training class, thinking perhaps this would be a good adventure. She was not at all prepared to stay in jail, and called her husband, who had no idea where his wife had been or what she had gotten herself into. He posted her bail, and I'm certain they had an interesting discussion on the way back to Fort Worth. The other women

were ready for whatever came their way; they were women of real GRITS (girls raised in the South). Their talk of a hunger strike and other methods of noncooperation stirred concern among the sheriff's staff.

The men in the group were a little easier going. Able to send messages to the women and to our support group via the deputies, we received books, notes of well wishes and updates from folks outside. Only one of our numbers, a volunteer/blockader from Austin, took independent action. He decided to express his solidarity with the women by refusing to wear any clothes during his imprisonment. While the rest of us supported his decision, we suggested minimizing his activity in the small cell.

I received the book, *Soul on Ice* by Eldridge Cleaver from Carobeth, who along with others formed our support group. They were the folks who were the lifeline to the press and the outside world during our lockup. I spent the weekend reading the book and doing a lot of soul searching on several levels. I thought about how I could continue my resistance work along with my career as a self-employed arborist. I was also facing the reality that this was my third arrest in less than a year. But there were higher priorities at hand—good food and drink. The first thing I wanted after leaving jail was a good cheeseburger and fries. Jail food was not good, to say the least.

Dallas lawyer Tom Mills provided pro bono services to us, as we were big in heart but didn't have deep pockets. He

$5 billion is just the beginning...
We'll still be paying for Comanche Peak 30 to 40 years from now.

Unless we act now to halt nuclear power in North Texas.

The cost of Comanche Peak will have risen from $780 million in 1974 to more than $5 billion upon completion in 1985. And we, the ratepayer/taxpayer, have paid the bulk of this expense.
Texas Utilities Company gave us fair warning back in 1977..."The System's 3 electric utilities placed rate increases into effect in late 1975 and in 1976. However, revenues and earnings were adversely affected by mild weather, conservation, inflation...We now face the task of obtaining additional rate increases,...to provide the higher level of earnings required to maintain our financial strength...The System's construction program is the principal factor."
From 1977-80 the TU System requested double-digit rate hikes, every six months to a year, among its member utilities. The majority went to finance cost overruns at Comanche Peak through increased CWIP charges (construction work in progress)...as much as 99% in 1979 and 89% in 1980, for Ft.Worth consumers.
When the plant is completed, don't expect your electric rates to go down. Studies predict that the generating costs of new reactors will average 20-25% more than those of new coal plants. We've only just begun to pay...

If Comanche Peak operates:
* Electric utility rates will skyrocket as the burden for operating the $5 billion plant falls heaviest on residential consumers.
*The plant, operating at 70% efficiency, will require about 200 tons of milled uranium per year. Fuel-cost projections are $29 million/1982, $53 million/1983 and $50 million/1984.

* Highly radioactive waste will be stored at Comanche Peak and then possibly shipped for reprocessing into nuclear bombs.
*There's no way of predicting costs of storing the highly radioactive waste material...prices can only go up, and we'll bear the burden in increased rates.
* We can expect to see significantly more cancers and birth defects throughout North Texas, including the D-FW area, from planned and accidental releases of low and high level radiation.
* The area from the Oklahoma border to below Waco will be threatened with a catastrophic accident that the government estimates would cause 6,000 deaths, 14,000 injuries and $117 billion in property damage, making the land uninhabitable for centuries.

And yet, under the Price-Anderson Act, Texas Utilities will be liable for only $560 million of that irreparable damage.
*Rate/taxpayers more than likely will pick up the multimillion dollar tab for dismantling the plant 30 to 40 years from now.

Comanche Peak Life Force wants you to be a vital link in the nonviolent fuel blockade and other peaceful protests we're planning this month.

*Come to organization meetings, Sundays at 6 p.m., 2710 Woodmere in Dallas. CALL (214)337-5885 FOR INFORMATION.

COMANCHE PEAK NONVIOLENT BLOCKADE

__ I endorse cancellation of Comanche Peak. __ Send me more information.

used the standard defense at that time of imminent danger. Those of us who lived in Dallas and Fort Worth gathered at his office a couple of times. The charges of criminal trespass were soon dropped, as Texas Utilities didn't want any more press involving protests.

We started planning the next action, fueled by the energy and support generated by the Road Gang barricade/blockade. The publicity of the action on the first anniversary of the Three Mile Island catastrophe gave the Texas anti-nuke movement a good boost as the news of the action spread.

CHAPTER VII
Zoo World and The Pentagon 1980

A local radio station, KZEW-FM (the "Zoo") put on a mini festival April 12 through April 15, 1980 at the Dallas Convention Center. The Dallas affinity groups signed up for a booth to encourage and generate support for the next action at Comanche Peak. There were bumper stickers, leaflets and buttons available for public outreach. Over 600 signatures on several petitions against nuclear power were gathered and later send to the main office of Texas Utilities. Wooden buttons were made from slices of dried pecan branches that I collected from my work as an arborist in Dallas. The buttons were unusual at best. I used an ink pen to write slogans on them, and a magnetizing glass (solar power) to burn the letters before adding a coat of epoxy along with a small pin clip glued on the back. The buttons were a hit and sold well, bringing in much-needed revenue. Tom Sherrill, a graphic artist,

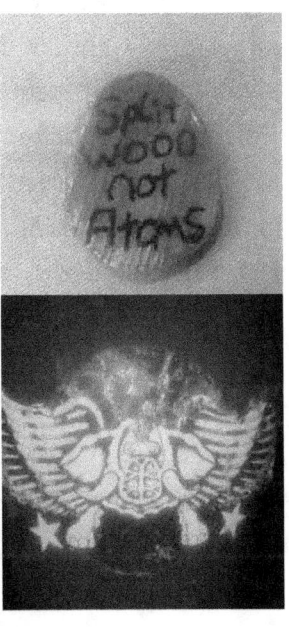

designed t-shirts and the bumper stickers which were sold to raise funds for the upcoming actions.

The Zoo World/KZEW radio station event helped get the word out about our actions and created a good rapport with the public. Many questions were asked ranging from the problems about nuclear energy or nuclear weapons, to off-the-wall questions like, "who is paying you guys to do this?" These were positive conversations with no hostility just back and forth discussion. Some questions arose about what was going to happen next for Comanche Peak Life Force. The answer was that it was up to the good citizens of Texas, and we encouraged everyone to get involved and help make a difference.

Sign-up sheets were available for those wanting to become involved. The required non-violent training before any action was very well received and helped initiate several discussions. Over 150 people signed up for the training classes plus many more were willing to support in different ways, such as gathering signatures and in fund-raising efforts. References to Gandhi, Dr. King, the Civil Rights Movement and the Farmer Workers Movement seemed to connect with the people earnestly interested in helping and being a part of history. The training classes continued throughout the spring and early summer for the action planned for July 4, 1980.

While non-violence civil disobedience training went on during the weekends, affinity groups around the state were meeting using the consensus process to make decisions about the upcoming action. Meanwhile, reconnaissance was being done on site at Comanche Peak. A few folks took night drives to the nuke, followed by long hikes onto the property gathering as much information about the terrain and lay of the land. This reconnaissance continued through the first of July.

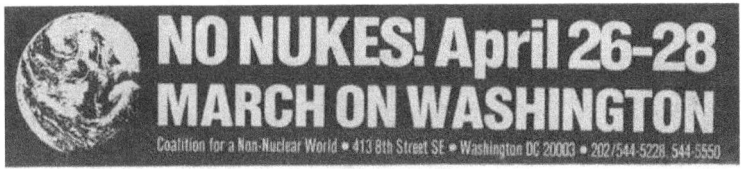

A national action was called for April 25, 1980. The event, an antinuclear weapons and antinuclear power action was organized by the Coalition for a Non-Nuclear World, and called for the shutdown of the Pentagon. After much discussion, a group of us from Texas planned to take a couple vans to Washington D.C. to participate. Some folks felt it would be a waste of funds and energy that could be used on the local level. Others felt the numbers were needed in D.C. to show the country, and the world, the need to stop the war machines—or at least slow the madness. The CPLF had a trusted person in Washington with an ear to the ground who kept us updated on the preparations for the rally. He had returned to Dallas after planning meetings in Washington to share the information. The plan was for us to stay at a local

"NOT LARGE
BUT SUFFICIENTLY ELEGANT".....

CHRIST CHURCH, WASHINGTON PARISH • Founded A. D. 1794
Washington's First Parish

church, sleeping on the floor and using their kitchen. After a long 20-hour road trip, we settled in at the Christ Church, Washington Parish and began to review the plans. A 31-page handbook was available which included maps, legal guidance and general information about this upcoming action. After sleeping on the church floor in sleeping bags or wrapped in blankets using backpacks as pillows, we awoke to fresh coffee and oatmeal.

We gathered on April 28, 1980—it was a cold rainy day, and we stood at the National Mall listening to a few speakers as we readied to march to the Pentagon. Some volunteers had already blocked workers access to the Department of Energy building about two miles from the Pentagon. Thousands of marchers in orange and black colored t-shirts, some wearing ponchos and rain gear, crossed the bridge over the Potomac River. Groups had previously volunteered to blockade the different entrances to the Pentagon as well as access to the other buildings.

CIVIL DISOBEDIENCE ACTION TRAINING HANDBOOK

MARCH FROM THE DEPARTMENT OF ENERGY TO BLOCKADE THE PENTAGON
APRIL 28, 1980

Coalition for a Non-Nuclear World
413 8th St., SE
Washington, DC 20003

202-544-5228

Under arrest at the Pentagon, 1978
Photo copyright 1978 by Dorothy Marder

$1

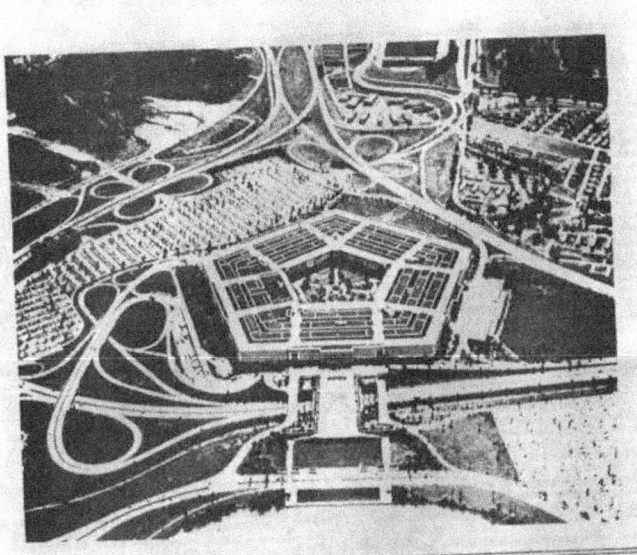

☐ Please sign me up for Nonviolence Training in Washington, April 27.

☐ Please send me information about training sessions in my area.

☐ Please sign me up for the April 27 Logistics Update.
(I've already had Nonviolence Training.)

☐ Please send me _____ Handbooks
(3 or 4, 50¢ each; 5 or more, 25¢ each).

A three color button of the design on page 31 is available:
1 to 9, 75¢; 10 to 99, 35¢
100 or more, 25¢

MARCH FOR A NON-NUCLEAR WORLD
WASHINGTON, D.C.
SAFE ENERGY
FULL EMPLOYMENT
HONOR NATIVE AMERICAN TREATIES
STOP NUCLEAR POWER
ZERO NUCLEAR WEAPONS
APRIL 25 · RELIGIOUS CONVOCATION
APRIL 26 · LEGAL MARCH and RALLY
Washington Monument
APRIL 28 · NON-VIOLENT CIVIL
at the Pentagon
APRIL 24, 25, 28 · CAPITOL HILL LOBBYING
Coalition for a Non-Nuclear World
413 8th Street S.E.
Washington, D.C. 20003
(202) 544-5228

Shut down the Pentagon

MARCH FROM THE DEPARTMENT OF ENERGY
April 28

October 21, 1967, Pentagon demonstration. Photo by Minoru Aoki.

If we are serious about our desire to achieve a non-nuclear world, then we cannot be content to limit our protests to a legal march and rally every few months. The government and corporations, who are so heavily entrenched in nuclear technology, will not dismantle their nuclear power plants and nuclear weapons without a determined struggle by the anti-nuclear forces and people of this country.

On the morning of April 28, we will gather at the Department of Energy (DoE) in an effort to leaflet employees and slow down the operations. The DoE is the only Federal agency which researches, builds, develops, and promotes both nuclear energy and nuclear weapons.

Because of the current and historical link between nuclear power and nuclear weapons, because the United States is the only country to have used nuclear weapons on people, because the U.S. has more nuclear weapons than the rest of the world combined, because the U.S. has advocated first use of nuclear weapons, because of the escalating Iran/Afghanistan crisis, we as anti-nuclear activists call on all concerned to join us in a march from the DoE to the Pentagon on April 28.

If we—who are so concerned about the escalating nuclear threat—are not willing to make sacrifices, such as risking jail,

"Go back to your communities and be willing to go to jail if it comes to that, because I'd rather see you in jail with the jails filled up than the graveyards running over."
Dick Gregory, Washington, D.C.
May 6, 1979

then how can we expect to convince the general public to take more moderate steps. Help us dramatize the nuclear danger. Put your body and convictions on the line. Join us the morning of April 28 at the DoE, then march to the Pentagon, and SHUT IT DOWN.

CHECK-IN	NONVIOLENCE TRAINING	LOGISTICS UPDATE	SUPPORT MEETING
one representative per affinity group	(for those not trained in civil disobedience)	(for those trained in civil disobedience)	(at least 1 from each affinity group)
544-5550, 546-6647, 544-5228	St. Steven's Church	Calvary United Methodist Church	All Soul's Church
Saturday, 6-10 PM	16th & Newton, NW	1459 Columbia, NW	16th & Harvard, NW
	Sunday, beginning at 1 PM	Sunday, 3 PM	Sunday, 3-5:30 PM

COALITION FOR A NON-NUCLEAR WORLD, 413 8th Street, S.E., Washington, D.C. 20003
202-544-5550, 546-6647, 544-5228

MARCH FOR A NON-NUCLEAR WORLD

April 26-28, 1980 · Washington, D.C.

April 26: Legal March & Rally
Washington Monument

April 28: Non-Violent Civil Disobedience
Department of Energy/Pentagon

Capitol Hill Lobbying · Religious Vigil White House

Coalition for a Non-Nuclear World

Stop Nuclear Power ★ Zero Nuclear Weapons ★ Safe Energy ★ Full Employment ★ Honor Native American Treaties

NATIONAL OFFICE
413 8th Street SE
Washington, D.C. 20003
Eastern Market Metro · 202/544-5228

LOCAL CONTACT
214-337-5895
817-261-1828

Holly Whitson's account of Shutdown the Pentagon and The March on Washington D.C.
April 28, 1980

For me, it all began with a flyer tacked onto a pole. The flyer was advertising an Anti-Nuclear March on Washington and an Occupation of the Pentagon on April 26-28, 1980. Having read enough about nuclear power, I was dead set against it, but I had never personally done anything about it. The flyer interested me; it might be an adventure and a way to learn and get involved. But honestly, had I not needed to go to the east coast, I might never have heard of The Comanche Peak Life Force. Little did I know that calling the number on the flyer would change the course of my entire life.

I needed a ride to the east coast because I wanted to get to New Haven, Connecticut and check out Yale Law School. I had been admitted a month earlier and had until early May to tell the school whether I would be attending or not.

Mavis Belisle answered the phone and explained the members of the Lone Star Alliance- an umbrella organization made up of various groups, including Comanche Peak Life Force planned to fill a van and ride to and from the demonstration in Washington D.C. There was a mass protest planned on the Mall for the weekend, and a civil disobedience action planned for Monday, and the van would return after the protest, and after anybody arrested got out of jail.

On the way, I learned about the dangers of nuclear power, the arms race, and uranium mining, the nuclear power plant accident at Three Mile Island, the Church Rock uranium spill near Gallup, New Mexico that had dumped radioactive contamination into the water supply, and the murder of labor activist Karen Silkwood, a Texan, who was killed for exposing the health and safety violations at a Kerr-McGee nuclear facility in Oklahoma. I learned about the construction of a nuclear power plant in Texas, the so-called Comanche Peak Generating Station. These protestor-warriors had been fighting the nuke for years and were now traveling around the country to get training in tactics for pulling off a direct-action occupation and to drum up support, hoping to motivate anti-nuclear protesters from around the country to come to Texas in the middle of the summer to take on Brown and Root, who was building the nuke, and the Texas Rangers who, it was anticipated, would defend the nuke against the occupation.

These beautiful people and the facts I learned about nuclear power and nuclear weapons stirred my soul. But here were young people who were sacrificing everything, changing their personal life stories to dedicate themselves to resistance that was necessary to quite literally save the planet. They also educated me about the organization of the resistance movement that (unbeknownst to me) I was about to join.

The central organizing principle was the affinity group. This was a model that had been employed in the anti-war movement of the 1960's and 1970's. It had been successful in a protest at the Ruhr nuclear power station in Germany in 1969 in which 30.000 people participated in the protest, "occupation", and blockade. Every anti-nuclear protest I attended in the early 1980's followed this model: while there might be tens of thousands of protesters at the demonstration, they were an amalgamation of small affinity groups. Affinity groups from a certain larger locality or larger organization might identify with a broader "Alliance- Clamshell Alliance, Comanche Peak Life Force, Catfish Alliance or the Natural Guard, but at their core organizational level these alliances were composed of small affinity groups.

The affinity group model was premised on the fact that a small group of friends would join, train together and allocate among each other the responsibilities for the success of the group and the upcoming demonstration. If group members intended to get arrested at the protest, certain members of the affinity group would be responsible as "support persons." To collect phone numbers of family members. To work on the outside to locate the arrested people. And to generally support the arrest action undertaken by the arrestee. If an affinity group chose to undertake "direct action: by blocking entrances to nuclear facilities, climbing the border fence and trespassing on site, or *in some other way, it was all the more important to work with a smaller group of friends. A group of say 20 friends going to a larger demonstration might all travel together and even stay together at the event, however, that group of 20 friends might constitute three or so affinity groups. We all knew each other and would certainly support the larger group but at our core we knew who was in our small group and that was our support, strength, and protection.*

The affinity group model was not only highly efficient, it was well guarded against infiltration by government agents, undercover police or - an even greater threat - undercover actors hired by the owners of the nuclear power plants themselves. The affinity group made such provocateurs and "agents" easy to spot. They came seemingly out of nowhere, claimed to need a group to attach to and tried to get to know the members of the affinity group and join their efforts. On more than one occasion, our Comanche Peak affinity groups warded off efforts by such suspicious persons to "crash" our group and tag along with us. We tended to handle the situation by saying nothing of any importance around the person and ensuring that the person was not invited to our group.

When we arrived in Washington, D.C. I was met with a sight that would change the rest of my life. We were greeted by misty rain, cloudy skies and perfect weather- not too cold, not too humid or warm.

Nobody cared about the gentle rain. Thousands upon thousands of protesters were teeming. There were colorful signs, some elaborately crafted and others simple poster boards with messages scrawled in black marker. Young people, old people, kids. Older people who had obviously been at such events before and young people like me who had never seen anything like this many people unified in their voices. Everywhere a sense of mission, of purpose, of what was possible. At this protest I saw for the first time - it wouldn't be the last- the Bread and Puppet Theater protesters, The Bread and Puppet Theater puppets were tall and made of paper mache and cotton puppets on long sticks. People poked the sticks up, up, up, and spoke their message not with sound but compelling images. Tragic expressions painted on paper mache heads, sweeping white fabric made capes and drapes moving in the breeze created by the movement through the crowd. Bread and Puppet theater brought signs, passion and stirring images to the protests. There were drums, cowbells, and noisemakers., along with protest songs and chants.

    We made our way to the speakers and singers at the rally. More facts, more passion, the power of truth. Hope even amidst such frightening information about how close our planet was to annihilation from the threat of nuclear war, radiation poisoning, and contamination to our water, land and air that will literally last for thousands of years into the *future. Helen Caldicott from Physicians for Social Responsibility describes the reality of the "launch on warning systems" for nuclear weapons that could be set off without human intervention, governments could believe the other side had launched a nuclear strike. People advocated "alternative energy", the only solution. Wind, solar, renewable energies, Native American women from the organization, Women of All Red Nations ("WARN"), who shared heartbreaking stories of children born with deformities and elders dying of cancer and leukemia because of radiation from uranium mill tailings that had contaminated water supplies and had been used in bricks to build houses. Bonnie Raitt and other musicians who had recently banded together as Musician United for safe Energy (MUSE) put music and words to the fire in our hearts. Regular people proudly sharing stories of their arrests at nuclear facilities around the country. With so many thousands of people and so many stirring speeches and music, it seemed like we really could change the world.*

Monday, April 28, 1980 was the day the group was slated to shut down the Pentagon, I did not attend that part of the protest. Instead, I took a train up to New Haven, Connecticut where I could look at Yale Law School, where I had been admitted to law school in the fall of 1980.

In the meantime, my friends from the Comanche Peak Life Force had participated in an assault on the

Pentagon, the goal was to shut it down. While that did not occur except for the helicopter landing pad occupied by Texans and some folks from Oklahoma, the demonstration was a success.

After the trip to Washington, I was hooked. I was going to change the world. I was going to do it with my new friends in the Comanche Peak Life Force. The next stop was Seabrook, New Hampshire.

—End of account written by Holly Whitson in 2020 about action in D.C. in 1980.—

Our Texas/Oklahoma affinity group had volunteered for the helipad on the north side of the Pentagon. Without much effort, we simply walked onto the landing pad and formed a circle, occupying it for the day. No choppers landed on our watch.

Blue Navy buses were brought in to transport those who were arrested. These buses were parked between the helipad and the main building, making it easy for us to do hit and run disruption maneuvers throughout the day. As some sat in front of doorways with linked arms singing songs of peace and resistance, others looked for ways to disrupt the daily comings and goings of Pentagon employees, even blocking the ramps from the Pentagon concourse to the Metro subway station. Not wanting to get arrested, it was more important for me to stay active and fluid, always moving from area to

area, setting up small barricades using whatever materials were handy and trying to let the air out of the Navy bus tires. Many who were arrested refused to post bail, which caused a problem with authorities as the jails were soon full with over 300 activists, marking the largest mass arrest of political demonstrators on a single day since the Mayday anti-war demonstrations of May 3 thru May 5, 1971 when more than 7,000 were arrested in downtown Washington. Our action was designed to show that large numbers of citizens do not support the actions of the industrial military mindset of corporate America. Few people in our merry band were arrested. They posted bail, as it was a long way from home to be in jail. We all participated in slowing the military madness in and around the Pentagon in Washington D.C. at least for a day or so. The trip back to Texas was full of reflection and stories of the past several days and planning for the next action against the proliferation of nuclear power.

CLAMSHELL ALLIANCE

The Clamshell Alliance exists to unite New England people about nuclear power and about safe renewable energy sources. Nuclear power plants are dangerous to all living creatures and to their natural environment. The nuclear industry violates the natural order of life. It is designed to concentrate profit and control in the hands of a select few, undermining basic principles of human liberty. The Clamshell Alliance opposes nuclear technology in all its forms.

Our alliance sprang to life in July of 1976 when nuclear opponents from all parts of New England met to develop a strategy for opposing construction of the proposed twin reactors in Seabrook, New Hampshire. It was clear that following eight years of local opposition the Nuclear Regulatory Commission, ostensibly a regulatory agency set up to protect public interests, would instead promote the Seabrook project by disregarding the time-honored tradition of home rule.

In response to the N.R.C. issuing a construction permit in Public Service Co. of N.H., the first of many public displays of opposition surfaced. On August 1, 1976 eighteen local citizens walked onto the proposed nuke site in the first collective act of non-violent civil disobedience in the history of the U.S. anti-nuclear movement.

With each successive demonstration the numbers of demonstrators grew — 180 resisters occupied the site in late August, 2,000 in October, 2000 in the following April resulting in thousands of arrests. Legal rallies drew over 20,000 supporters from across the nation. The tactic of non-violent direct action shaped other groups nation-wide to follow the same footsteps of Clamshell activism.

The 4th of actions of nuclear resistance in New England has mobilized itself on a variety of issues. Focused public opposition has been instrumental in the cancellation of plans to construct a second nuclear plant in Plymouth, Mass. Seabrook II lies still on the drawing boards and the completion of Seabrook I so seriously in doubt. A combination of political and economic pressures, legal environmental opposition and enhanced awareness on conservation and alternatives to nuclear power have stopped the industry in its tracks. Not a single fission reactor has been ordered since 1976.

The Clamshell Alliance remains steadfast in its efforts to halt further construction at Seabrook. Three major chapters (Merrimack Valley, Greater Newburyport and Seacoast) maintain contact with safe energy and pacifist groups throughout the region. The direct relationships between nuclear power and nuclear weapons have broadened both our focus and our repertoire of tactics. We support electoral campaigns, lobbying agencies of government, legal matters, rallies, educational programs and we advocate the full participation by an informed citizenry in any decision that may affect our health, safety, liberty and economic security.

It is in this spirit that we applaud the efforts of artists and musicians who appear on this recording. We celebrate with them the spirit of our movement and pledge our continued support and fellowship. Together we stand in defense of life — for ourselves, for our neighbors, and for all future generations.

CHAPTER VIII
Seabrook 1980 and The Eyes of Texas

The Clamshell Alliance formed in 1976, organized to carry out actions of nonviolence against the nuclear industry at the Seabrook nuclear power station. Clamshell had several occupations resulting in nearly 2,000 arrests, helping to keep the anti-nuclear message in front of the American public by way of national news via newspapers, tv and radio.

The Seabrook nuclear power station in Seabrook, New Hampshire, was the site of the first and largest demonstrations and civil disobedience against nuclear power in this country. More direct action against Seabrook was to occur in late May 1980. A group of volunteers from Texas joined with several thousand protesters at Seabrook, finding themselves at the point of the spear in the action. After a day of fruitless encounters with authorities, the police had used tear gas, riot sticks, dogs and fire hoses to keep protesters from occupying the site. The occupiers retired and licked their wounds as they planned for the coming dawn. The Texans crept into the darkness of the Atlantic coastal night and returned at dawn carrying a roll of the nuclear plant's own cyclone fence and singing The Eyes of Texas Are Upon You. That small fence-cutting action brought new life to a stunned occupation and

Come to the
FREESTATE
in Seabrook, New Hampshire

the
Organizing Community
for the
May 24th
OCCUPATION/BLOCKADE

Coalition for Direct Action at Seabrook

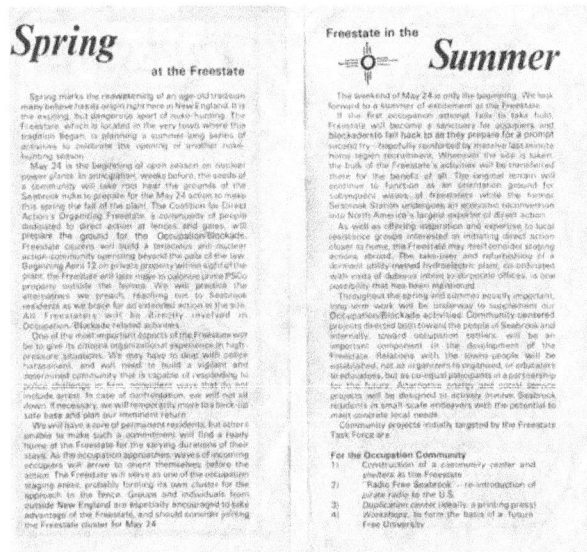

continued the legacy of Texas anti-nuke resistance that had spread from coast to coast in a short period of time. It is worth noting the possession of bolt cutters/wire cutters in Texas is illegal. The national media was ever-present and they covered the actions in an unbiased way. Those of us back in Texas were able to follow the action via tv and newspaper reporting as well as an occasional phone call. While cutting the fence was a symbolic, yet brave, act, it gave thought as to why we should destroy fences or property at all? Why throw tea into the harbor or dump subsidized produce on the ground? The reply was, in order to stop the nuclear madness (nuclear facilities) we must put ourselves in danger and literally tear the fences and buildings down before they become useful to the profit-makers.

Posing with the loot of fencing on the railroad tracks leading to Seabrook, the Texans, along with a few thousand

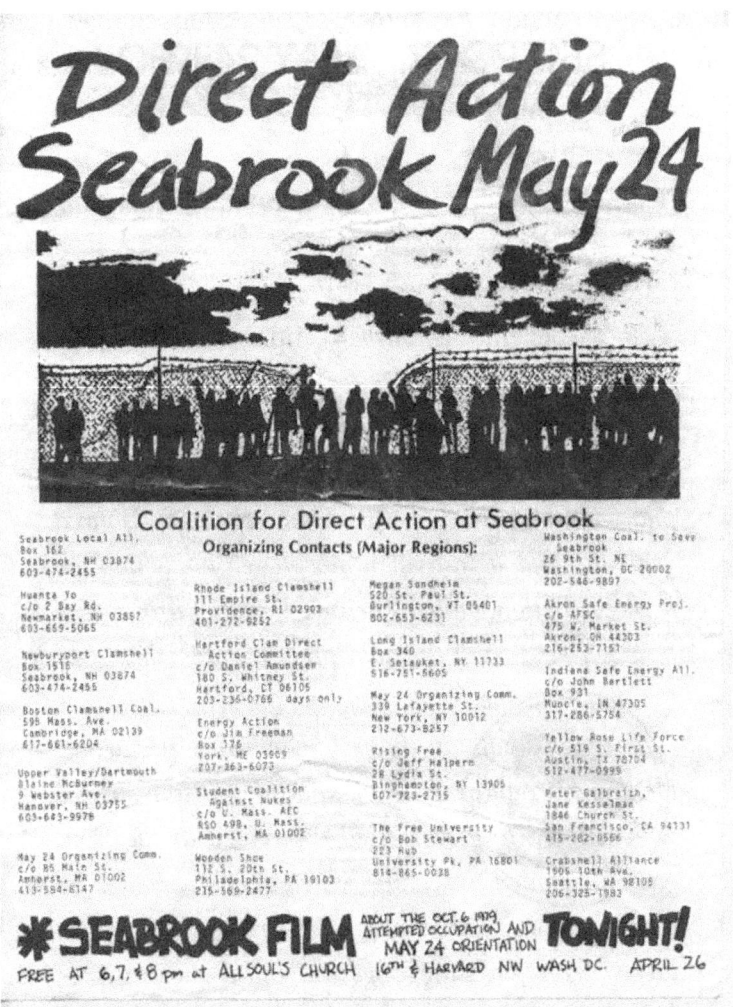

volunteers who showed their determination to protect the planet and their country from the proliferation of nuclear power. Their stories would fuel the fires of direct action across the country. Upon their return to Texas, information gleaned from mistakes made and the knowledge gained from small victories were shared at potluck dinners and on scouting runs. Again, action was shown to speak louder than mere words. These were tree hugging patriots and fence cutting volunteers of America.

Holly Whitson's Account of Seabrook Occupation May 24-27 1980

In 1980, the Clamshell Alliance was widely regarded as the crème de la crème of organizations fighting nuclear power. The Clamshell Alliance affinity groups did not mess around. They were not planning a rally, with inspiring speeches, shared granola, and a festival atmosphere. Implementing a direct action model borrowed from Europe. The plan was to assault the nuke on two fronts; there was the action at the front gate, and then there were the "pop-up" assaults on the perimeter fence at various locations around the heavily guarded facility. Those who wanted to get arrested assembled at the front gate, blockaded the road—which of course had been closed anyway for the protest—refused to move, locked arms, and sang songs until those who could not be persuaded by tear gas to disperse were eventually arrested, carried to school buses and carted away. Those who did not intend to get arrested (or who preferred to actually trespass on site and get arrested inside the perimeter fence) assaulted the outer fence armed with bolt cutters to cut the chain link fence, makeshift ladders for scaling the fence, handcuffs *to lock themselves together once inside, and crude protective gear. The protective gear ranged from regular bandanas sometimes drenched with water to mitigate the sting from the inevitable tear gas assault and gas masks purchased at Army Surplus stores where we bought almost all of our clothes and gear, to tin cups some of the men slid their private parts into under their pants to provide some protection from the merciless strike of the batons.*

The confluence of the two groups was at the front gate. Affinity groups that had focused their efforts on the perimeter fence would return to the front gate, proudly waving around like a prize the sections of the fence they had procured and the big heavy bolt cutters that had facilitated the deed. This taunting with the sections of the fence, combined with the direct-action protestors' refusal to join the "we-are-now-sitting-in-the-getting-arrested wing" infuriated those guarding the nuke, who lashed out with high pressure water hoses, tear gas and rough manhandling of the protestors (hair pulling, shoving, dropping them on the concrete, etc.). The protests at the front gate were relentless, brave and messy. Those waves of arrestees, sometimes in larger groups and sometimes just a few locked together, bravely sat through the water, tear gas and insults thrown their way until they succeeded in making the police haul them away. All the while, the support people, protestors who did not want to get arrested, spokes, peacemakers and facilitators, all chanted, sang, and yelled support for the arrestees. The occasional appearance of someone taunting the authorities by waving chunks of freshly-cut chain link fence would cause great shouts of glee from the protestors and great frustration from the police who could do little about that without diverting their focus from keeping the others from getting too close to the front gate.

The thing that has stuck with me all these decades about the Seabrook occupations was the helicopters. All night, the helicopters would buzz the protest camp. Thump, thump, thump. Chop, chop, chop, chop. cling-cling-cling-cling...back and forth. They accomplished their purpose; it was impossible to sleep through. But for me, more than the exhaustion, it was the fear that has stayed with me all these years. Since those days, Seabrook was not the only direct action where helicopters buzzed the protestor's camp, I can never hear a helicopter without a tiny lightning bolt of panic, a jerk, a startle that makes me retreat inside, away from the windows. Every time, I remember those sleepless nights and the feeling that the struggle we were having with the nukes and those who built them was real, not theoretical.

One needs only to look at the protestor camps to fully understand what being at these protests meant on a practical level. Some sympathetic nearby landowners had permitted us to camp on their property, so apparently there was not much the police could do about that. But this was not glamping. If anyone in an affinity group was lucky enough to have a tent, it was filled with as many people as might fit inside. Most of us simply lay down in our clothes, using our army-surplus packs for a pillow. We didn't leave our items at the camp during the day's festivities. My group didn't have cars, we had caught a ride from Texas to Seabrook and would hitchhike back. So barely sleeping with the helicopter noise and lights going all night, whatever we had brought with us was shoved into our backpacks and carried around with us all day long for fear that the camp might end up being raided. There wasn't a lot of room for clean clothes or much of anything else in those tiny backpacks. People who were ultra-prepared had goggles to fend off the tear gas, extra bandanas to be used both to conceal our identities and to flush tear gas out of the eyes and of course bicycle locks to affix protestors to the fence or to make more permanent the "doorways" they made in the fence. Also gloves, bolt cutters, or other implements the person might want to bring was the equipment of the day.

Not everyone concealed their faces with bandanas, but many did, including me. In our direct-action training, we learned that the company "goon squads" photographed protestors and shared the photos nuke to nuke. We knew federal agents were taking pictures. If you saw someone taking pictures, you assumed they were with the nuke or the feds or some other *person who meant us harm. At least in the direct-action circles, taking photos was considered rude for that very reason. Those who were going to sit in the road and get arrested usually didn't try to hide their faces, but many if not most, of the direct-action people did so.*

Our fear was not theoretical, it was real. While few were afraid of getting arrested most of us were afraid of being separated from our friends and something bad happening to them. (Remember this was decades before cell phones existed.) We were afraid of pepper spray in our eyes. We were afraid of the stinging force of the hoses. We saw people bloodied and didn't know if it was rough treatment they received, or they simply cut themselves on the fence or what.

Part of what made our fears more real was the sacrifice of the anti-war protesters who were just a few years before us on the timeline of American resistance. In some ways, their cause had been more immediate; the young men were literally being forced to report for duty, stuck on planes and flown off to Vietnam from where they returned in body bags. They fought hard wherever they were, including draft board offices, recruitment offices, main streets and college campuses. On May 4, 1970, the Ohio National Guard shot unarmed anti-war protesters at Kent State University, killing four of them. Those images of dead students lying on the campus ground amidst their friends had been seared into my memory as a teenager and they were not lost on me as I watched waves of us approach the front gate and present ourselves for fire-hosing, tear gassing and other quite real painful tactics used by those defending the nukes.

At all our protests they were there. The anti-war protestors who had seen all this before and were keen to government infiltration, provocateurs sent into our mist to foment violence in order to give us a bad name and justify the increasingly violent measures used against us. The feminists were there also, and in these demonstrations the seeds of what would become the Eco-Feminist movement were planted. The Yippies and the Anarchists and the "Nobody for President" devotees were there. All of them returned to the streets to share with us what had happened to them, what had worked and what didn't, why they fought so hard and why they were proud that they stood against the war machine. I thought the grief of what they lived though, their lives shattered by the anti-war movement they had to be part of, sending them into hiding on organic farms out in the country never to be seen in activist movements again. I have always harbored my own grief for their loss, for our country and courts being turned over to mean conservatives, the gentle spirits having spun into an unrecognizable drug fog or a cult or the corporate world just when it had seemed real change had been within their grasp.

I was wrong, many of these activists had never

"left" at all. They came to continue to speak the truth, breathing wisdom into the anti-nuclear movement of the 1980s just as determined as we were that our future- our planet's future- had to be one without nuclear power, without a nuclear arms race without hatred.

—**End of recollections by Holly Whitson, written in 2020—**

Kent Wilson's Account of Seabrook Occupation May 24-27 1980

I couldn't say if the railroad tracks blockade was part of the plan when we set off for the back forty of

the Seabrook site, bolt cutters in hand. I'm sticking with that story. Our small group of about fifteen people mostly were Texans who sort of knew each *other from antinuke protest actions back home.*

What I did know was that we traveled a long way from Texas with the intention of "occupying" the Seabrook nuke which was under construction.

The Clamshell Alliance opposition went back years. Now nonviolent direct action was proving a challenge. Lots and lots of law enforcement, from every state around.

From camp I had scouted around a bit. So had the guys organizing this little adventure. They had found a great spot to cut the fence and get on site (technical occupation! Also known as trespass). So, we set off, following a nuke supply railroad track to a relatively remote area around the side.

We lay hidden in the grass, watching the fence. On the inside perimeter road, a security guy passed by about every seven minutes. Our little band of Texans were going to occupy Seabrook.

This ad hoc group mostly knew each other, we came up from Texas to join the Clamshell occupation of the Seabrook nuke, still under construction. And when we set off for the back forty of the Seabrook site, bolt cutters in hand, our goal was simple, get on site.

The reality of getting 'on site' at the main entrance was not looking great, despite monumental the multitudes hammered at the gates but were pushed back by water cannons, pepper spray and batons. It was a melee, an experience beyond the relatively mellow occupations thus far in Texas. At Comanche Peak a hundred protesters was a small victory; at Seabrook there were thousands. Longtime widespread opposition to the Seabrook nuke set this stage. Nonviolent direct action was proving a considerable challenge to anti-nuke activists and law enforcement alike.

Following a rail track skirting the edge of the nuke property brought us to a somewhat remote spot where we would try to enter. We figured to cut an opening in the chain-link fence, step inside, trespass and then get out of sight before the guy in the pickup drove back by.

After setting up a lookout on both sides, the bolt cutters went to work. Two people would run up, cut a few links and then hustle back into hiding. The guard in the truck passing back and forth never noticed. Once the opening in the fence was large enough, we moved quickly. One or two at a time, most of us ran up and stepped thru, did a little victory fist pump, said no nukes and headed for cover.

This completely symbolic action had us all feeling pretty righteous. Then somebody suggested a piece of that fence might make a good blockade somewhere. This action slightly more challenging, had potential. A quick consensus meeting and with no one strenuously objecting, the bolt cutters went to work. Meanwhile the security guy would drive by every few minutes, and so far, he had not noticed a thing. Even when a large piece of the fence was dangling by a couple of links. Soon there was a hole about five or six feet long in the fence. The piece of fence that we had dragged out of sight as the truck rounded the corner.

He stopped and stared at the opening. He got on the radio. "There's a big hole in the fence. It's just gone. It was there a minute ago!" Mostly true, I was certain he would see or hear us now, but he drove away, still talking with his people. We dragged our trophy back along the railroad track, clippety-clop. The track was rough, the chain link was heavy. At one rest stop someone suggested we leave the fencing right where we were. To interfere with the supply train that used the track, but that didn't pass consensus. Thinking that might be dangerous, (I couldn't disagree with that; I was also thinking that splitting atoms to boil water or level cities is also dangerous.)

Traipsing into camp with our little roll of 'Seabrook fence' attracting a bit of interest. Rumor has it as a good contribution to the cause, being quite a boost to morale.

We stayed in camp to rest and prepare for the next day, again supporting the main action at the front

gates. We occupied Seabrook.
—*End of recollection of action in 1980, written by Kent Wilson in 2020*—

CHAPTER IX
July 4, 1980

The stage was slowly being set and ideas were shared on how we could make the occupation of Comanche Peak on July 4, 1980 an action to be remembered. The nuclear plant sat on over 4,000 acres making finding access easy. Topographical maps and good old riding the backroads proved useful for getting the lay of the land. The affinity groups from the metroplex, including Dallas and Fort Worth were doing most, if not all, of the scouting of the various points of access to the property. The eastern and southern sides had been thoroughly mapped in our minds from precious scouting, eliminating the need to put into writing points of access. Night hikes around the property were carried out regularly without the aid of flashlights. The lighting from the construction of the nuke and occasional moonlight was more than enough light to make our way down the gravel security road. In all four directions large metal transmission towers some still under construction while others completed brought power into the plant. The gravel road, wrapping around Squaw Lake, was easily accessible.

As your eyes adjusted to the Texas darkness each night

there was always some interesting encounters with wildlife, everything from jack rabbits, roadrunners to small herds of whitetail deer. It was easy to walk down the roads around the nuke property, always on the lookout for security trucks, which didn't have a real timetable for patrolling the perimeter of the property. When headlights were spotted, a quick warning was sounded and into the ditches and tall grasses we dove, careful to avoid the prickly pear or pencil cactus. For some reason, the rattlesnakes, spiders, scorpions and horny toads never presented a problem, perhaps because they sensed we were all in this endeavor together. No Nukes!!

Climbing the large metal transmission structures gave a sense of the magnitude of what we were up against. The fact is, large amounts of electricity are needed in society, but the question was and still is at what cost?

Some of these scouting runs were productive in that as it was not uncommon to find left or dropped wrenches at or near the base of the highline towers, perfect to loosen bolts within reason or just a couple of turns (yea right) or to damage the threads of bolts which were embedded in the large concrete piers poured for the base for the new towers. These daring and risky climbs offered a view of the surrounding terrain which amounted to mesquite and cedar trees fifteen to twenty feet tall. Thick groves of mesquite and cedar trees can be traced back to over grazing and the cattle drives of the 1800s when the native grasses were consumed and trampled by the herds of cattle. The mesquite beans were a favorite food of these beast and were spread northern as the native flora could not outgrow this onslaught.

Stands of live oak trees were spotted and duly noticed as potential rest areas or campsites for future actions and occupations. Live oaks grow as single trees or in clusters of a dozen or more. Clustered trees range in size from four or five inches in diameter to large ones of maybe ten or more inches. They are great for hanging hammocks and providing

Civil Disobedience is Civil Defense

COMANCHE PEAK BLOCKADE

FOR A NUCLEAR-FREE TEXAS

Join us in a training and preparation session for nonviolent direct action

SUNDAY JUNE 26 1:30-6 p.m.
2710 WOODMERE DALLAS

**THE FUTURE IS NOW
WE ALL LIVE IN GLEN ROSE**

COMANCHE PEAK LIFE FORCE   214-337-5885

cover if needed. The larger single trunked live oaks with low arching branches are easy climbs and provide great views of the surrounding terrain.

The scouting runs also served as a source of inspiration and team building which can only occur from real action rather than just sitting around talking about doing something. Our scouting teams ranged from two to four members and the cars used in transport were small economy models with good gas mileage. Focus shifted to the north and northwest parts of the property where it seemed large numbers of occupiers could enter the property with little chance of being detected.

Little or no new fencing was being placed around the outer areas even though new cyclone fencing was going up within a half a mile from the two reactors. There were a few outlying sheds used to store tools and large water coolers. These were valuable resources during the reconnaissance missions, even though we carried enough water for each outing in canteens or bota bags' worth per person, which usually lasted at least several hours. (A bota bag is a traditional Spanish liquid receptacle used mainly as a wineskin made of leather.) Knowing about the water coolers and having access to them was a cool advantage, sometimes the coolers still had ice inside. The water was always taste tested before drinking. Experience helps, if a cooler was polluted, the "off" flavor taste is always there. That's a skill I learned growing up in the South and drinking out of water hoses in the summer.

Small herds of white-tailed deer along with jack rabbits and an occasional roadrunner were our companions and comrades during this time. Every now and then a wary coyote would be seen, and like the coyote, we learned to hit and run away, able to strike another day. It thus the Kiote became our spirit animal.

Daylight missions were a bit more involved, since the recognizance was done on foot, we had to be dropped off and picked up later at a different location. I always enjoyed it

when it was my turn to be the driver. I would drop a team off on the northern perimeter, then drive to Granbury, passing the time walking the sidewalks and discovering neat shops in this beautiful little Texas town. The first of July came quickly, as did the adventure that lay before us.

The actions at the front gates on United Way on July 3, 1980 seemed more of a festival than an occupation. There were no blockades or sit-ins with locked arms. It surely gave the authorities reason to remove their white hard hats and scratch their heads. A large water tank on stilts was visible off to the side of the road just inside the completed cyclone fencing. The tank had NON-POTABLE WATER printed on the side and with a nice metal shed stood next to it. Our guess was that the shed held fire hoses and pumps and maybe a generator for the water in the tank. Hosing down protesters quickly came to mind since this tactic had long use against nonviolent protesters. But there was peaceful guitar playing, songs being sung, and folks holding banners and waving signs. There was no reason to break out the water hoses.

This peaceful event continued throughout the day. The CPLF was making a statement which would show citizens of Texas and America, we do not want or need this nuke. While the small festival-like demonstration was going on at the front gate, about ten of us were already camped on the property of the Comanche Peak Steam Electric Station. We had already been on site for several days with enough supplies to last about a week. We had been entering the property from the north for a couple of days. We knew more supplies could be brought in at any time with the shuttles carrying more occupiers or from groups hiking in to participate in the encampment planned for the next day at "Camp Liberty Hill," the quickly christened occupation site. Hammocks were hung among the live oaks, and dark brown and green clothing was the camouflaged uniform of the early occupiers. The supporters outside the main gates wore the infamous bright red t-shirts of the CPLF. In the towns of Glen Rose and Granbury, it was easy to spot a protester because of their clothing. In all, there were at least a couple hundred people who came in for the occupation.

The prep work paid off in more ways than one. The Dallas Morning News reporter Elna Christopher had come to realize when told we were going to make a statement of some sort; we were true to our word; it was going to happen. That was certainly the case in the days to come. The general feeling among the affinity groups on site was one of near revolutionary zeal. We knew it was going to be a good action. Previous large occupations had been greased but not this time. All prior contacts involved either Hood or Somerville County Sheriff's offices, made through the legal representatives of the Comanche Peak Life Force.

The continued dialogue via the press informing the public of our nonviolent civil disobedience tactics was an invaluable strategy. Those of us involved in the action felt in our hearts we were doing the right thing in opposing the construction of the nuclear plant. It gave us mental strength and resolve that is hard to describe. The night of July 3, 1980 was one of great anticipation. Plans had been made to show a presence as the sun was rising and warming the sky. We didn't want to start too early however, as to allow enough time for the support group at the main gate to be in a festive mood. Late arrivals came onsite before dawn and were briefed on the coming events. Items including a large parachute, several Colonial and early American flags and banners made for the event were ready to be unfurled at a moment's notice.

A nice open area among the cedars and mesquite trees was chosen for our stand on Liberty Hill. This spot was about a quarter mile from the last campsite of the occupiers. Other sites had been secured and were stocked with water and food, consisting of trail mix and survival bread, no plastic wrappers and no glass bottles, except for one special bottle of mead. The mead was provided by activist, author and fellow prankster, Albert Most. We stored the mead in a small hole, basically a ground refrigerator that I had recently dug. It was a hole about one foot wide by eighteen inches deep and lined with small stones. That allowed the contents to remain cooler than the air temps above ground, and in Texas in early July that ranged from low 90's to above 100 degrees. The Texas summer of 1980 didn't let us down.

We received word that the Texas Rangers had been seen in larger-than-usual numbers in both Glen Rose and Granbury, which gave us some pause. The Rangers had long used the motto of "One ranger, one riot." Our current action, and all previous CPLF actions, had been far from riots, as we were all schooled in non-violence civil disobedience. Yet, their presence in the area presented an interesting turn of tactics by the powers that be. The Texas Rangers had been providing law enforcement in the Texas territory since 1823

and probably had enough information to warrant this larger-than-normal showing.

Friday, July 4, 1980 was a good day of protesting, a festive display of community in defiance of the construction of the nuke. At least one hundred people had gathered at the front gates carrying on conversations with locals, the press and

others who drove out just to see what the fuss was about. There were conversations about safe alternatives to nuclear energy and about how we all live close to the nuke (no matter how far the drive to get home). Singing songs and carrying signs, the protesters left authorities wondering what was going on. In previous actions members of the CPLF climbed the fence and were quickly carted or escorted away via the yellow school buses. This day there were four buses, but no ladders and no effort of the citizens gathered to break the law. The gathering continued much as the day before with no real threat of forced removal by guards

July 4, 1980 marked the fourth day of what was the longest occupation of a nuclear power plant property west of the Mississippi River and one of the longest in the history of nonviolent civil disobedience on United States of America soil. The sun broke the eastern horizon with a beam of light and warmth to be remembered for a long time by the two dozen or so folks who had either been on site for several days or had hiked in during the predawn hours. The stage was set as a parachute tent was erected along with the flags of '76 being unfurled with banners declaring this site occupied until further notice.

The activity at the United Way Drive gates was festive, yet subdued, for there was an air of anticipation, knowing the action was about to unfold. When asked by the media what was going on the spokesperson for the CPLF replied with a simple statement that the property of The Comanche Peak Nuclear Plant had been occupied since Tuesday, July 1, 1980 with a presence actively established at Liberty Hill.

This was about 8 or 8:30 a.m. with the Texas sun bright and shining, just like the white ten gallons hats of the Texas Rangers and the white hard hats of the plant security guards. As if someone had kicked a fire ant mound, the helicopters readied for takeoff. The media ,who had their own chopper, were also biting at the bit to get something on tape for the evening news.

Those of us at Liberty Hill were using no walkie talkies, so we attempted communicating at a distance with others onsite with bird calls. It became obvious the was going to be interesting, to say the least. The four or five of us acting as guides (wearing black armbands for identification) were familiar with the terrain which consisted of uneven rocky ground, shrub oaks, patches of prickly pear cactus and a few large mesquite trees scattered among the fifteen to twenty-foot cedars, waited as things began to get stirred up. The sounds of several helicopters taking off in unison certainly grabbed our attention. We readied to communicate with hand signals and bird calls, and the deer trails that had become our paths quickly came into play.

It had been decided ahead of time who among us would be voluntarily arrested and who would try to avoid capture and continue to occupy the site. The reconnaissance work done in the weeks and months prior would pay off, both now and in the coming days.

As a Caracara Eagle stalks a covey of quail, the Department of Public Safety chopper with Texas Rangers aboard rose and landed in what seemed less than a heartbeat, as the media chopper started circling the area looking for a good photograph or two.

Folks wanting to be arrested formed a circle and quietly waited for their fate. This gave time for the rest of our peaceful rag-tag group of volunteers to scatter. The guides, with several folks following, spread out in different directions. The DPS chopper dropped off several of the Rangers to deal with the occupiers at Liberty Hill and had quickly returned into the air in hot pursuit of the rest of us. Camo makes a world of difference, as most folks who venture outside much would know. Hunters and anglers realize "hiding in plain sight" is the way to go. And once you've been looked for in broad daylight by a chopper hovering just above the treetops at maybe fifty feet, the phrase takes on real meaning.

For me, the sound and dust from the chopper came way too close for comfort. This was not right, why were they

on our trail so quickly? My guerrilla instincts felt there had to be a reason, a red flag or something. Quickly spotting one guy wearing an old red CPLF t-shirt gave me my

answer. He had decided not to get voluntary arrested at the last moment.

Quickly having him change into something less colorful, then stashed his red shirt under a rock to take the heat of the chase off my pack of Kiotes. With an incredible adrenaline rush, we were able to hustle downhill toward Squaw Creek Lake and to the safety of our basecamp. Meanwhile, seven people were arrested at Liberty Hill. The TV crew got their footage for the evening news, and the newspaper photographer Jay Godwin captured some good pictures for the *Dallas Morning News*. It was during the arrests that the cactus dragging incident took place. Jim Schermbeck was deliberately dragged through a large patch of prickly pear. This act of unkindness resulted in several thorns being deeply embedded and having to be surgically removed later. Jim was later ordained into "The Order of The Prickly Pear."

The photo shows eight Texas Rangers and a helicopter along with several protesters being led away and others on the ground near the infamous cactus patch. Those folks were taken to a well put together holding pen in one of the parking lots close to the plant. The detainees were held there for the remainder of the day with no shelter from the sun

The summer of 1980 broke or tied 29 daily heat records—42 days straight of triple digit temperatures. Twice in June the temperature had hit 112 degrees. The temperature was well over 100 degrees on the 4th. We knew

the cost of our actions and the cost of safe clean energy wasn't going to be cheap.

Later in the afternoon the arrested protestors were taken to the Hood County Jail in Granbury. After being held overnight, five members of the CPLF were released on $200 bond each. The two remaining patriots chose to remain in jail because it was against their personal conscience to pay out bail money for the charges of suspicion of criminal trespassing.

A game of "cat and mouse" continued throughout the next several days with little to no direct contact with the Rangers or Sheriff's department. The Texas Rangers and the Texas Utilities security guards weren't well prepared for going into the brush and it seemed as if they didn't really care to chase anyone, which enabled spokespersons on the outside to speak with the media about why the occupation was continuing and why CPLF occupiers were there for the long run.

The authorities immediately and often denied there were protestors on the property, and they continued that line throughout the two-week occupation. We were ever vigilant of our location and knew what the ramifications of our action would be. Yet there was a lack of concern by the authorities about trespassers on the property of a nuclear power plant under construction.

You can use a lot of energy hanging out in a hammock listening to the birds and thinking of verses to the next song. The caches of water and nonperishable goods came in handy. Mosquitoes weren't much of a problem, insect repellent picked up at the Army surplus store and a homemade citronella

swipe kept these flying buzz saws at bay. Yet chiggers seemed to make up for the lack of mosquitoes. There were no fire ant mounds rising out of the rocky ground, but the pesky insects managed to find us. The trail mix we carried consisting of nuts, dried fruits and berries seemed to be a favorite of fire ants, any open bag of food was a target. Leaving food on the ground for this would quickly turn into an ant picnic.

After a couple of days, the occupiers and supporters were both ragged and worn. It was the hottest summer in memory, and while quick swims in Squaw Creek Reservoir helped cool things off, it only gave momentarily relief to the real reasons we were making this stand.

Holly Whitson's Account of July 4, 1980

It was during a life-threatening heat wave on July 4, 1980 that the Comanche Peak Life Force launched its assault on the Comanche Peak Nuclear Power Facility in Glen Rose, Texas. We prepared for weeks, really for months. In reconnaissance missions performed in the middle of the night for weeks, the occupiers had scaled the fence and tramped around the site making a mental map. Potential camping spots were selected that had maximum potential to hide us. Potential weaknesses in the internal perimeter fence close to the nuke were identified and feasible trespass routes were selected. Water jugs, matches, pencils and paper, Texas flags and other supplies were stashed.

These weeks of site reconnaissance were not the only preparation. The CPLF had been with the Lone Star Alliance and Mobilization for Survival (MOBE), fighting this nuke for years. There had been training in creative nonviolence, peacekeeping, personal safety and of course, scientific aspects and medical risks of nuclear power.

At least one of our ranks, Ken Nelson, had gotten a job at the nuke where, for months, he had been part of a construction team that had free reign at the facility. He mapped it carefully inside and out. He drew detailed sketches, he knew the facility, its surroundings, shift schedules, staffing levels at various work locations and the like. He learned where all the most important construction equipment and parts were located. This information would prove to be invaluable as we came up with specific targets and tactics for the monkeywrenching planned for those long nights on site.

In the middle of the night before the July 4th occupation, my affinity group of about five people was driven to a location far from the internal security fence for drop off. We would walk to our pre-planned location much closer to the internal security fence— an eight-foot-tall chain link fence. At our drop off point, the only thing preventing our entrance onto nuke property was a four-foot barbed wire fence and a "No Trespassing" sign. We had gone over that fence many times before but this time it was different. We were going in to stay there. And people who did not mean us well would be trying to find us.

While we hoped to evade capture, we were not stupid. We figured we would be rooted out and arrested in short order. As we looked around our tiny band of occupiers, we did not know who among us might not make it. But we knew that whatever happened, every single one of us that could evade capture was going to stay on site. We also knew that many other affinity groups were in the same boat, crossing the fence and headed towards the nuke's internal security fence.

We arrived at the drop off point about 2:00 a.m. It was already 90 degrees. While the moon wasn't full, it was plenty bright which was good, because needless to say we could not use flashlights for fear of being detected. If we could last the weekend, the moon would be dark and stay that way for ten nights. Little did we know at the time that our occupation would last weeks, not days.

The entire well-rehearsed drop off procedure took only seconds. The driver cut off her lights, pulled over and out and over we went, quickly scaling the barbed wire fence, then running as fast as we could to the mesquite brush that would hide us from passing cars or security patrols with their spotlights. Once safe, and after a group hug, we began our hike towards the nuke through the scratchy Texas brush.

In part because of that scratchy, poky, unforgiving mesquite brush and in part we were in the thick of rattlesnake country and had barbed-wire and chain link fences to scale, we were fully geared up head-to-toe with thick U.S. Army camouflage clothes and heavy shoes. This was no time for summer picnic clothing. We needed to hide in the trees and brush, we needed to look like the trees and brush.

The insects were as thick as the searing heat and even more oppressive. The mosquitos were awful, but the chiggers were worse. Chiggers are tiny, an almost invisible bug in the spider family. People call them "red bugs," "harvest mites" or their scientific name, "trombiculid mites." They put out an itch so bad you could scratch the skin off your legs trying to make it go away. Our best cure was usually pouring bleach into the bites but that's a really bad idea for a lot of reasons and we couldn't do that because we were living on site, without luxury items like bleach. The chiggers were worse than the Texas Rangers, worse than the 112 degree days—they were the worst of the worst. To this day, I have a permanent chigger-bite scar on each of my shins, each about the size of a nickel. They are gouges I wear proudly and gratefully as a lasting memory of the Comanche Peak Life Force occupation of July 1980.

During those long hot days, we barely moved. Near each other but not right next to each other, we nestled into the trees, a few feet up off the ground in hammocks, where the foliage was thickest. Moving in the dry brush inevitably made noises so we didn't. We didn't talk, we used hand signals, an occasional bird call. We didn't move we didn't breathe heavy if we heard so much as a twig crack. Those of us with eyeglasses had to take them off for fear that a reflection would catch the eye of one of our hunters.

The contrast was striking, the security force (when they wanted) thundered through the brush, talking, hollering to each other, breaking twigs as they crashed along. We could hear them coming well in advance of them passing by us. Once, two men just a few yards away from me. This scenario was repeated every day but didn't last long in the heat of the Texas summer.

The days belonged to the pursuers for what little they did, the nights belonged to us. After a safe interval after dusk, my affinity group reconvened. We dug our jugs of water out of their hiding places (sometimes, sadly emptied or destroyed by our hunters). We had "dinner," — usually some hard tack (survival bread) that Sally Mitchell had made or sometimes can of Spam or Army field rations. The fuel tabs and matches were used to heat coffee or whatever mystery meat we had (labels didn't hold up well). We laughed, shared stories from the day's adventures and near captures and passed out "stick joints" holding our breath with each toke and pretending we were getting high, with each pass of the "joint" making it more real. I swear sometimes it worked.

After we buried our scraps of trash, it was time to get to work. Nights were busy and never seemed long enough. The goal was to scale the inside security fence, get inside the high-security areas and make our presence known. That might be as simple as scattering and hiding pipes and other construction supplies we found, tearing away plastic covers and dumping water on items subject to rust, bending things that would bend and breaking things that would break or other minor acts of monkeywrenching. More often it involved getting close to the nuke and making huge piles of items that belonged elsewhere, spelling out "solar" or "no nukes" with construction supplies or affixing and laying Texas flags here and there. The idea was that upon the dawn both those who worked at the nuke and the news helicopters would see our handiwork and then could not deny that we were on site and certainly could not truthfully say we had not penetrated the high-security areas inside the internal fence.

A short word about feminism and the role of women. Women were the backbone of the organizing effort and in every respect treated as equals by the men. We were all in this together. In that way, the women were freed from the history we had heard about. The sexism that was rampant during the anti-

war movement, in attitude and practice, did not exist for us. There was no difference between our women and our men. But on the ground, we were faced with a stark potential line: the eight-foot fence. Not all my sisters went over that tall chain link fence. You know who you are, and as a woman we share a special bond for that reason. The low barbed wire was one thing. But to get over that tall chain link fence with the equipment we were carrying sometimes required a "hoist" whether the climber was a male or a female. Maybe more women had an understandable aversion to having other people hoist us—literally, shove our

Task Force on Women + Nuclear Energy
2110 WarAMen
Dallas TX 75233

Hello -   3/6
  I am working on a research project dealing w/ women's involvement in the anti-nuke movement. I am particularly looking at the strategies women use to make themselves heard, connections between feminism + anti-nuclearism, + the political history of the movement + the women in it (ie, links w/ the Left, Civil Rights movement, anti-war movement)
  I'd greatly appreciate any resources or ideas you might have.
                          Thank you
                          Helen R. Graves
                          116 3rd Ave
                          Santa Cruz CA 95062

butts up as we scrambled over. Whatever it was, the relative scarcity of female fence-scalers didn't change the importance of the women's role or their risk taking, or our acceptance by the males in the group. Perhaps because fewer women scaled that fence, they predominated in the public face of the organization and in its nervous system. They were the media spokes, the organizers, the facilitators at the front gate; the seeds of the "eco-feminism" movement of the 1980's which would in short order take off with the Women's Pentagon Action in November 1980, the Greenham Commons Women's Peace Camp which launched in 1981, the Seneca Falls Women's Encampment for a Future of Peace and Justice which began in 1983 and lasted for four years and an explosion of women's anti-nuclear and anti-war organizations, reflected in the Lone Star Alliance, Comanche Peak Life Force, Mobilization for Survival and other organizations. As women led, organized, designed and implemented tactics and strategies, liaisoned with the press, conducted affinity group training, got arrested, engaged in direct action in the middle of the night and yes, scaled that formidable chain link fence with the guys all while some of them were already raising small children.

We knew that Dallas Power and Light was not going to close construction at Comanche Peak based on our occupation. We realized this nuke would probably get built, but hopefully it would be one of the last.

In the meantime, we had work to do on site. The sun would give way to a dark night sky, the temperature would dip below 95 degrees and we would roll into action mode for the time to monkey-wrench.

Most of the time our creative disruption amounted to unspoken communication with the powers that be at the nuke. It was private and unseen by anybody but us and them. They knew we were there, but they were quick concealing the fact from the public. Early in the morning the workers quietly removed any symbolic evidence of our presence, like our "No Nukes" banners. We left evidence that plainly saw, like when we cut the razor ribbon wire on the fence to get over it or when we spelled out no nuke messages with their piping or swiped the keys to the tractors when they were careless enough to leave them out of locked areas. Within a day or two after the demonstration launched on July 4th, the spokesmen for the nuke were announcing publicly that we were all gone and that any stray demonstrators were very far from the high security areas if they were on the property at all. That was never true, and those people knew it. We had unfettered access to the high-security areas throughout the two-week occupation. Of courses, we didn't hang around there during the day but at night it was still our playground.

—**End of account written by Holly Whitson in 2020—**

CHAPTER X
Making Our Presence Known

It was decided a sign of defiance or of determination was needed to let the world know the CPLF was on site after over a week and still active. Plans were made for the event and steps had been put into place to make this happen. Our press contact, Elna Christopher, was notified that a presence would be shown at daybreak on Tuesday, July 8, 1980. With two of my trusted friends (Ken Nelson, alias Albert Most, and Jenny Gregory) we decided to carry out this part of the action. Jenny was nimble on the trails and good at communicating with bird calls along with being a dedicated anti-nuke activist. Ken was the alchemist in the group and had provided the mead and now the smoke bomb, which would help rekindle the flames of the CPLF resistance. He is also the author of *Bufo Alvarius*. Our excitement rose as we knew there would only be one good opportunity to make a true statement. Because the trails had been scouted and hiked so many times, the way was clear. Before dawn, we carefully made our way around cactus, rocks and low-hanging mesquite branches.

Settling in on a peninsula that jutted out into Squaw Creek Lake, we readied ourselves for the sunrise and the press we hoped would provide the coverage needed to show the presence of the continued occupation by the activists onsite.

The sun rose and quickly warmed the Texas sky. Anticipation grew as we were about to venture into new territory of nonviolent direct action. In the distance we heard the sound which is not easily forgotten. One I had heard at close range only a few days before, the sound of chopping air produced by an approaching helicopter. Not knowing who the passengers were on the copter, we hoped it was folks from *The Dallas Morning News,* our contacted media outlet. As the helicopter neared the plant site, we readied

ourselves with a couple of wide-eyed smiles and a wink. Having a vague exit plan (don't get caught), Ken lit the fuse, and within a few seconds the smoke bomb went off, the column of smoke rising several hundred feet into the air. While we didn't know it at the time, it made for one of the coolest photos ever taken at an action of civil disobedience.

Almost immediately we heard trucks speeding up and down the gravel roads which circled the outer areas of the 4,000-acre plant. We made our way southeast, knowing this was the closest way off site, but it was as if the fire ant mound had been kicked. Security guards had us surrounded. We were caught in a grove of live oaks with a thicket of sumac growing underneath. In a move that I later regretted, "Run you guys!" came out of my mouth. I was hoping my quick thinking of stashing my camera would go unnoticed, yet the camera was destroyed.

The guards were pissed off, to say the least. Two of us were handcuffed with cable ties and roughly dumped into the bed of a pickup truck. When asked "how many are there of you?" I responded with a sarcastic answer of "a few dozen." Not what they wanted to hear, and I was rewarded with a swift boot kick in my side. This act of frontier justice made breathing difficult and with the temperature of the truck bed hot as hell, we were hauled out. Jenny, the lookout of our band of pranksters, was placed in the cab, while Ken and I bounced in the hot truck bed. The pain in my ribs and the heat of that baking truck bed was memorable and our unwillingness to cooperate didn't help to chill out the guards any. I barely recall hearing over their radio one of our pursuers' trucks had

overturned while heading in the direction of the chase. The driver was not injured but learned not to speed and to always wear a seatbelt. His haste didn't matter, we were already on the way to the catch pen or so it seemed. My cohorts were taken to the Somerville County jail in Glen Rose.

Barely able to catch my breath from busted ribs I got from the security guard's kick, I was taken into the belly of the beast (the air-conditioned first-aid office of the company nurse), right next to the twin domes still under construction. This was as close to the nuke as I would ever get, with no real way to get loose and possibly occupy a room. After being given a cold bottle of water then examined, my official diagnosis was heat exhaustion. Never mind the boot kick in the side still hurt like hell.

I was transported to Glen Rose in an unmarked white sedan driven by a Somerville County sheriff's officer, dressed in classic Texas lawman clothes: Tony Lama boots and a Stetson hat. His stern, angry look was all the communication needed. After placing his unholstered 911 automatic pistol on the seat between us, any idea of escape disappeared completely.

In Glen Rose, with no mention of the smoke bomb or the ongoing action, Jenny had been released, with a ticket for trespassing. The outlaw prankster Ken Nelson was detained for not cooperating. At the jail, I signed my name and was released. I had been in the Somerville County jail before, and I repeated my tradition of finding a cheeseburger, a joint, some cold beer and a place to crash. Our violent handling by the guards was reported in the papers, creating a small distraction from the occupation, yet it provided a good opportunity to further the discussion about the reasons we were opposing this plant with nonviolent means.

The statement of the smoke bomb rekindled an ongoing debate about whether occupiers were still on site and active, and it made national news. Texas Utilities spokesperson and the DPS had been denying any of the protesters were still on site. At the same time the smoke bomb was set off, banners were unfurled at several locations on plant property showing a continued presence and more actions were sure to follow. By using the media as a vessel to share information we felt the public needed to know the dangers of nuclear power, from the mining of uranium to the yet unsolved problem of nuclear waste storage.

Supplies were replenished and volunteers came and went from the site. The occupation continued for another four days with no contact with the authorities except for a quick show to resistance by planting an American flag on the eastern side of the perimeter fencing. This was carried out via a canoe trip across the lake at night by some of the last occupiers. With spirits high and a feeling of accomplishment, a tactical retreat was organized and in true guerilla form it was implemented. No more arrests were made, and the jailed occupiers were released on their own recognizance. This prolonged action is still the longest nonviolent act of civil disobedience occupation at a nuclear power plant to date.

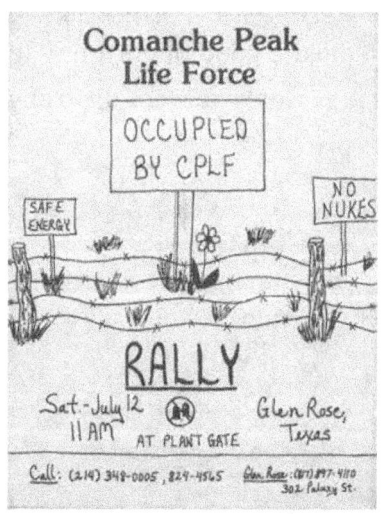

Local peer pressure was placed on the owner of our staging area just south of the Paluxy River. The electric power was turned off and the water was disconnected. It seemed as if we had worn out our welcome.

CHAPTER XI
Post Occupation Blues

The occupiers and supporters returned to homes across Texas and Oklahoma to begin reflecting and building on the results of our actions. The occupations had been successful in putting the issues of Comanche Peak Nuclear Plant in front of the Texas public. We began to ask ourselves tough questions, such as were the actions symbolic gestures and were different strategies with more creative tactics needed?

CREATIVE NONVIOLENCE

The two Dallas affinity groups merged into one group for several reasons. Some people were not ready for a prolonged struggle, others saw the fight against an industry supported by government subsides as a cautionary tale like Sisyphus pushing the rock uphill. Yet most importantly there was the need to pool ideas and energy. The adrenaline and positive energy brought forth from precious actions was strong and heartfelt. Also, the realization that we were doing battle with an industry which did not care about waste, toxicity or long-term consequences, only continued profits bore a heavy burden. The anti-nuke movement across the country and in

Europe that helped us create a series of events in Texas that had been seen and heard around the world. We were proud to have stood with our sisters and brothers at these actions.

As passionate as the volunteers were after each action involving weeks or months of planning and preparation, a strange sense of group loneliness would settle in. Although we were in the fight together, we were basically alone. The war to save the earth as we know it would be a lifelong battle, one skirmish after another. Post occupation blues is real and at the same time so was the desire to keep the struggle alive. Each day brought a new opportunity, it was up to each of us to make the most of the challenges and continue through the fog trying to earn a living while continuing the resistance.

Our small cadre was rolling, we began brainstorming about creative civil disobedience

in all its beauty. Another hit was always on our minds and the offices of Dallas Power and Light were front and center. We had learned much in the past couple of years about quick hit and run actions, posting leaflets, building barricades and forming human chains all under the shield of nonviolent resistance. These tactics had been studied and practiced during the Suffragist movement, at Seabrook in the east, to Diablo Canyon on the west coast, in marches throughout the South. European civil disobedience actions had been helpful in ideas and ways to disrupt construction and transportation means in and around nuclear sites, both weapon silos and nuclear power plants.

In Dallas, Texas Utilities stockholder meetings were targeted for ways to keep the No Nukes message out front. With some stockholders questioning the need for a nuclear plant and others more than happy to just receive dividends, the work of stirring the pot continued. Trying to draw attention to the cause was serious work but also a good way to overcome the blues.

Guerrilla theater was certainly one way to garnish attention. A black casket carried by two grim reapers along with zombies handing out leaflets during lunch hour raised a few eyebrows. Folks walking by with looks of wonderment made for a good audience, some willing to talk while others could not care less.

The spring of 1981 was a time of growth for the group

Request for support

May 15, 1981

Texas Utilities shareholders' meeting

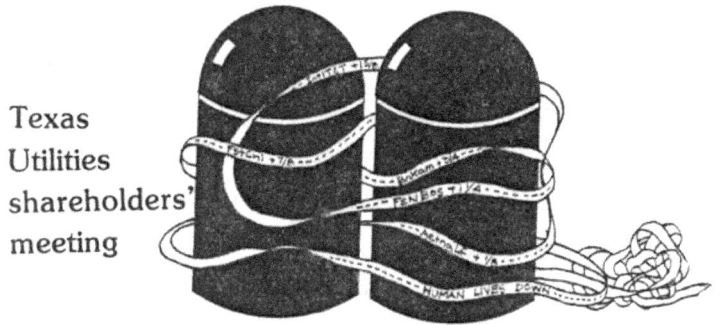

Texas Utilities is a major industrial conglomerate building the Comanche Peak nuclear power plant near Dallas-Fort Worth. Among its top ten stockholders are Dupont; First National Bank, Detroit; ITT; First National Bank of Boston; First National Bank, Chicago; Aetna Life Insurance Co.; Bankamerica, and Prudential Insurance Company of America.

The representatives of these corporations and many more will converge on Dallas for Texas Utilities annual stockholders' meeting, tentatively scheduled for May 15. The Comanche Peak Life Force will also be present. We'll be attempting to focus attention on the fact that folks in our part of the country are being forced to provide healthy dividends for out-of-state interests while we take all the financial and safety risks associated with the construction of Comanche Peak.

Since Texas Utilities is a national, if not international, company, we're asking safe energy groups across the country -- and particularly where the top ten stockholders are headquartered -- to target May 15 for some type of action to correspond to our demonstration in Dallas the same day. These actions could include anything from a noon hour leafletting and/or picket to small acts of civil disobedience. The type of action is not as important as Texas Utilities stockholders' knowing they've been targeted and receiving at least some pressure to withdraw their support from the company or support resolutions calling for the conversion of Comanche Peak to a biogas energy plant.

Since Texas Utilities is such a large and diverse group of interests, only a coordinated demonstration on many fronts will bring our point across to those who need to hear it most. We need and want your help in May. Please contact us for more information about Comanche Peak, and the upcoming stockholders' meeting.

Comanche Peak Life Force
2710 Woodmere Dallas, Texas 75233

in East Dallas. A couple of babies were born, and a large community garden was planted. Mavis was the only homeowner, the rest of us were renting homes in the East Dallas area. A vacant lot (with the owner's permission) created a place to practice newly learned organic methods of growing food and providing a place to share ideas about upcoming actions. The group was diverse, with people employed as carpenters, church workers, graphic designers, airline workers and arborists. There were moms, students and midwives, making for an interesting bunch of people. Having a couple of potluck suppers every week helped build bonds and keep the blues at bay. We were entertained by a merry band of musicians within our group. They would play as the rest of us enjoyed their songs of trouble and joy. I couldn't carry a tune in a bucket but wrote a ditty or two. "Sitting in my hammock writing this song. Wishing all you people had come along. No Nukes, No Nukes, No Nukes around here."

CHAPTER XII
Diablo Canyon September 1981

The Abalone Alliance was an anti-nuclear group that existed between 1977 and 1985 in California. They sent out a call to action for volunteers to help in the blockade of Diablo Canyon, another steam electric nuclear power plant near Avila Beach in San Luis Obispo County, California. The Abalone Alliance had been fighting the Pacific Gas & Electric's construction for several years. Thousands of folks have always shown up at their protests and were ready to support or be arrested again in the struggle to stop this plant from going online. Celebrities had been involved in the anti-nuke movement for a long time. Jackson Browne chose to be among those crossing the fence and being arrested as a member of the "Guardian Ion" affinity group. The nuke is located only three hundred meters from the Shoreline Fault which could produce up to 6.5 magnitude earthquakes.

We had been in contact with the Abalone Alliance via letters and long-distance phone calls. Holly Whitson, one of our warrior sisters, attended law school at Yale and being a

lifelong pot stirrer, her networking enabled communication with the groups on the east coast, Texas and the west coast keeping us updated on current events.

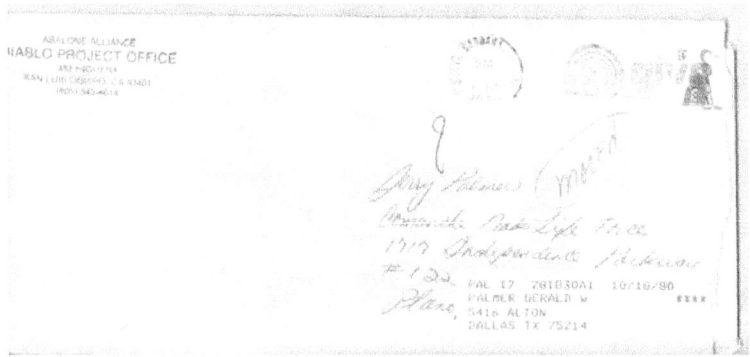

The blockade was planned for September 1981. Our small group agreed that we would attend and represent the fine folks of Texas, in particular the CPLF. We assumed our presence would be welcomed and appreciated, for word of the occupations and barricades/blockades carried out by the CPLF were known across the country. The summer came and went, not nearly as hot as 1980, but a Texas summer, nevertheless. Three self-employed radicals (Jim, Kent and me) with the support of the East Dallas group, prepared to make the trip west. We were to drive and our sister-in-arms, Holly, who was in New Mexico at the time, would fly in. The over sixteen hundred-mile drive took the better part of two days. We made the trip fueled by coffee, survival bread, water and burgers, and drove in shifts as we headed toward the Sierra Nevada mountains. The mountains came into view like a large dark cloud stretching across the horizon, looking as if a blue northern (legendary storms that

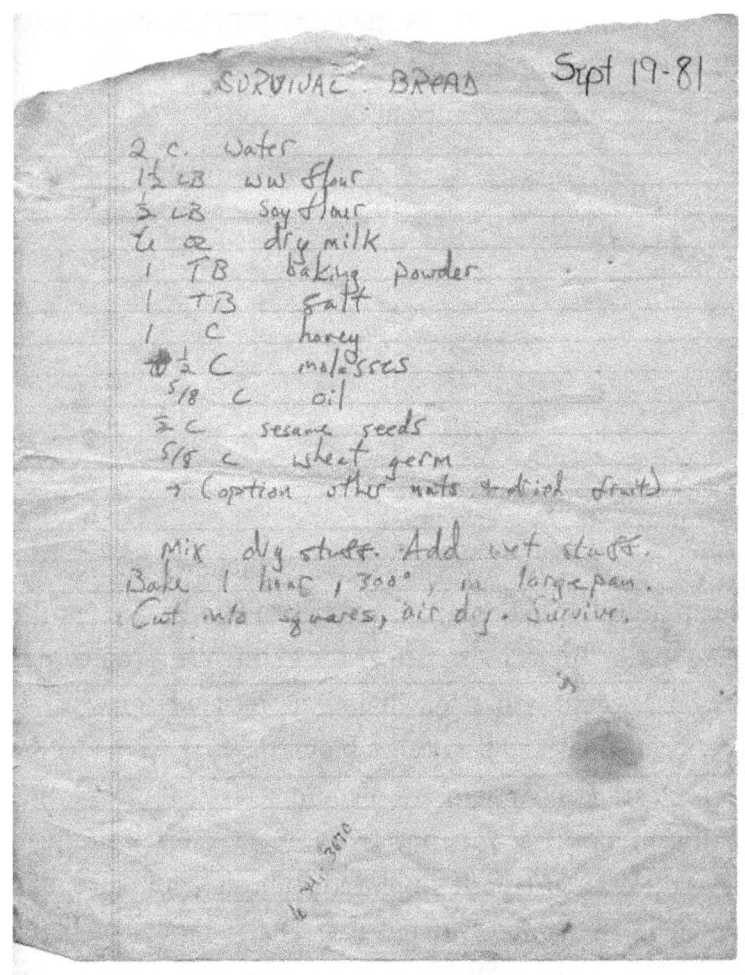

dropped temperatures thirty or forty degrees in a matter of a few hours), was just ahead. The decision to drive over the mountains, hoping to save time, was not the best idea. This short cut was an adventure to say the least. These mountains were quite taller than any I had traveled before. The Smokies, while impressive, just do not have the sheer cliff faces of the Sierra Nevada mountains.

GOALS OF THE ACTION

1. The blockade is not symbolic but is intended to actually obstruct the operation of the plant, and will be sustained for as long as necessary.

2. Increase the public's awareness of the serious dangers and drawbacks inherent in nuclear power, and the specific dangers of the Diablo Canyon plant.

3. Express the depth of commitment of many concerned people who say NO to nuclear power and YES to a sane energy path.

4. Assert the right and capability of everyday citizens to participate in the formation of our energy future in the face of the intransigence and irresponsibility of utility companies and the federal energy bureaucracy.

5. Assure that Diablo Canyon never operates as a nuclear reactor.

Declaration of Nuclear Resistance

We are committed to a permanent halt to the construction and operation of nuclear power plants in California. Nuclear power is dangerous to all life. We encourage the real alternatives of conservation and safe, clean, and renewable sources of energy.

To achieve these goals, we join together from throughout the state to form the Abalone Alliance to oppose nuclear power through nonviolent direct action and education.

Beginning with the Diablo Canyon nuclear power plant, our nonviolent action will be directed to all existing and planned nuclear plants in California. We will continue until nuclear power has been completely replaced by a sane and life-affirming energy policy.

We recognize that:

1. The much advertised need for nuclear energy is derived from faulty and inflated projections of consumption based on a profit system hostile to conservation. The United States has 6% of the world's population consuming over 30% of its energy resources. With a rational energy policy and appropriate changes in construction, conservation, and recycling procedures, the alleged "need" for nuclear energy disappears.

2. Nuclear plants are an economic catastrophe. They are unreliable and inefficient. Nuclear power is an extremely capital-intensive technology. In contrast, conservation and solar-related energy technologies will create many more jobs, both permanent and safe, than the atomic industry could ever provide.

3. The centralized nature of nuclear power takes control of energy away from local communities.

4. There is a direct relationship between nuclear power plants and nuclear weapons. The export of nuclear reactors makes possible the spread of nuclear bombs to nations all over the world. The theft of nuclear materials and the sabotage of nuclear facilities pose further threats to our lives and civil liberties.

Arriving at the headquarters of the Abalone Alliance, a small house in San Luis Obispo, we got signed in, and bought some swag: t-shirts, buttons and bumper stickers. We then headed to the staging area at nightfall and crashed in the car. We woke to an impressive tent city set up and run by the volunteers of the Abalone Alliance. The Abalone Alliance had taken the name from the tens of thousands of wild California

Red Abalones killed in 1974 when the unit's plumbing had its first hot flush of water. The staging area was buzzing with people of many different nationalities, ages, skin tones, hairdos and more styles of clothing than I could imagine, with reggae music playing on boom boxes. I noticed an odd-looking fellow—after studying him for a moment I realized he was "River the Rainbow child" who had gone off on the photographer in Glen Rose after the jury decision on Mavis Belisle's trial on trespassing charges. After a cautious hello we began to focus on why we came west. The fourth member of this rag tag bunch of Texas volunteers, Holly, had met us just as we prepared to leave the staging area. She was a welcomed addition, a true friend full of spirit and encouragement, always upbeat and honest.

Catching the shuttle van to the action about ten miles away, we ended up at a huge demonstration at the front gates of Diablo Canyon. We decided to watch the protest, literally thinking aloud how with some group cooperation we could easily blockade the entrance to the plant with materials within sight. But being in such small numbers and not wanting to cause unnecessary chaos we opted to head out to the activity occurring onsite. It was interesting being part of large numbers of like-minded people, much like the Pentagon a year earlier and being witness to how movements are built. The strategy of the Abalone Alliance was to clod the jails and court system with enough people to cause the general public to demand a halt to the construction of this plant. The facts of being on a fault line and the total cost of $13 billion seemingly would cause more than just casual concern.

We jumped into a shuttle van with our packs along with a half dozen others and rode into the countryside close to the northeastern corner of Pacific Gas & Electric's property.

Literally dropped off in the middle of the road, we followed our guide as we stepped into the underbrush. A well concealed trailhead led into the coastal forest. While

SEA BLOCKADE

The Sea Blockade is considering blockading the small harbor with boats, blockading the intake pipes with people in the water, and by landing blockaders on the beaches near the plant.

People who consider taking part in the sea blockade should realize that there is some risk involved, and carefully weigh their own abilities in a boat and in rough water. Each sea blockader must be able to swim 10 laps in a 25 yard pool and tread water for half an hour (without gear).

There will be one or more large boats provided to take people to the cove near Diablo Canyon. Rafts or smaller boats will then be used to ferry people nearer to the shore, probably inside the breakwater near the intake pipes of the plant. CB radios will help to keep communication going between the boats and rafts. It is very important for "parent" boats to keep lists of all people on small boats and their medical needs.

Affinity groups taking part in the sea blockade should have an even number of people, so that they can pair off as "buddies". There should be no more than 8 people in each sea blockade AG.

Each boat of any sort must have a competent captain or skipper. What he or she says concerning navigation, operating the boat, and safety measures must be respected as final.

IN-WATER TRAINING

Special training sessions will be set up in each region for affinity groups who plan to take part in the sea blockade. A qualified senior lifesaver will lead the group in exercises at a swimming pool while blockaders are wearing full wetsuit gear. Some exercises may include role plays of a panic situation, life-saving techniques, and methods for getting in and out of boats with gear on. There should also be a talk on safety and weather conditions.

In addition, ocean training sessions of 3 or 4 hours are recommended to get experience for swimming in ocean water, through kelp beds, etc. To set up one of these sessions, ask your trainer for the contact person in San Luis Obispo.

Fog hides the reactor as demonstrators approach it in their raft. They are watched by a PG&E security boat. August 7, 1978.

not the Texas hill country, the terrain was impressive, with large oaks covered in vines and flanked by ferns and other plants. Only later did I find out the huge vines, some the size of my arm, was poison ivy. There was some hasty talk about routes onto P.G.& E's property and we were quizzed about our nonviolent training, which in my opinion was a bit late, as we were already embedded in the action. Considering that several hundred people had already hiked in, only to cross the inner perimeter fence to be immediately arrested (sheep to the slaughter), a sense of calm prevailed. In total over two thousand people would be arrested in the two week long blockade.

Holly, the fourth member of this rag tag bunch of Texas volunteers, met us right before the van left the staging area. A true friend full of spirit and encouragement, Holly was always a good addition, upbeat and honest. After a ten-minute hike we approached a large clearing surrounded by small coastal live oaks and sheltered above by large valley oak. Resting here for a while and planning what to do next, the laid-back attitude of some of the activists surprised me. They had done their scouting over years and were comfortable about how to get onsite from many different locations. Not wanting to get arrested, our tactic was to hike in and establish a campsite on the property of P.G.& E., doing some scouting and supporting those who hiked in to cross the property line to get arrested. Finding a grove of trees wasn't as easy as it would seem, the terrain was steep. Hiking meant putting one foot in front of the other, steps taken were nearly waist high and then other times it was your foot in front of your face. Deciding on a spot just off the trail with several oaks growing up out of the California chaparral, we set up camp.

In hills ranging from

1,500 to 2,000 feet, dropping something or falling out of the hammock meant a rolling drop of at least 75 to 90 feet or more. It was from this precarious perch we carried out scouting hikes, always on the lookout for the authorities, also in constant contact with the herds of protesters headed to the fence in the valley near the twin domes of Diablo Canyon. Over a small ridge was a plateau within sight of the nuke, here leading to and from the nuke were the huge metal transmission towers which brought power in for the construction. The towers were the same as those around Comanche Peak. The difference was the cracking and popping sounds coming from the power lines. A bluish white light emitted from the lines was visible after sunset. It is no wonder they are considered a major fire hazard. For two days living on Sally's survival bread, trail mix and water gleaned from those headed to be arrested, we walked and escorted folks up and over the nearby ridge. Some made the journey

several times—having a good legal team enabled them to get out of jail and back to the protest only to be arrested at other locations along the property line. Singing a few stanzas of The Eyes of Texas seemed appropriate and added a little levity to the serious undertaking. Removing a Pacific Gas and Electric property sign for the folks back home in Texas only seemed appropriate.

The third morning, we were awakened by hikers, seemingly under duress running past our camp, followed by the unforgettable sounds of a chopper approaching from the direction of the nuke. Not overly concerned, as the trail had been cleared of hikers, it soon became obvious the location of the route from the woods to the main trail had finally been discovered. We stayed frozen as the chopper pilot slowly crossed the valley then turned and came toward the hill we occupied. Hovering perhaps several hundred feet below us, the helicopter was rising slowly only a few yards at a time. Looking down at helicopter blades is not something I will ever forget. As the chopper rose, and its occupants searched the hillside, we were soon eye to eye. The pilot's expression never changed. Once again, our camouflage protected us. Not seeing us, he lifted and flew the helicopter up and away from our camp. Smiling and with just a nod of our heads, thinking "well done, hiding in plain sight had worked again."

Hiking out that afternoon and preparing for the trip back home, we knew our solidarity with our sisters and brothers against the Diablo Canyon nuke (another monstrous waste of money and resources) had been shown. With many stories to be told, we returned to Texas after dropping Holly in New Mexico. This had been an inspiring road trip, yet I returned with more questions than answers.

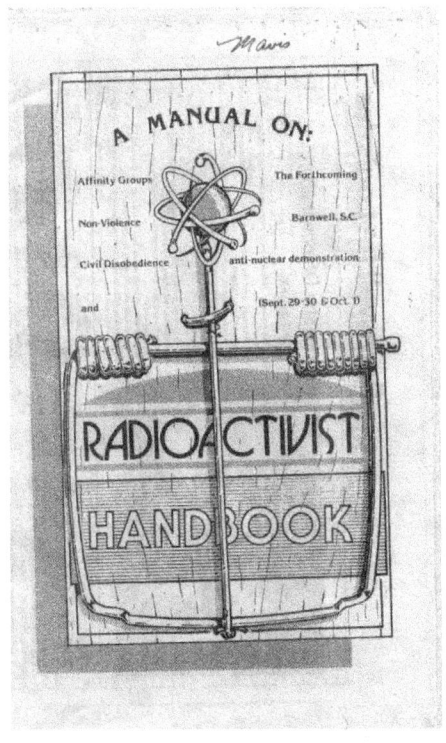

CHAPTER XIII
Bringing the Battle to Them via The Paint Bucket Brigade

Texas, while being a fiercely independent-minded state, did not have many people who were willing to attend protest rallies, carry signs and chant slogans. The only time they gather in large numbers is for football games or Willie Nelson 4th of July picnics. Our group was always brainstorming ways to come up with more ideas for civil disobedience in order to get the anti-nuke message out to the public.

We figured that banging on the front door might get their attention. About daybreak on September 23,1983 our affinity group paid a visit to the downtown offices of Dallas Power and Light, one of the partners in the Comanche Peak nuke. To bring more attention to the cost overruns, shabby

construction practices and the ever-present question of what to do with the nuclear waste from Comanche Peak and all the other nuclear plants in this country. We planned this to be a mock closing of the DP&L building at 1506 Commerce Street in Dallas, Texas. It turned out to be an actual closure that lasted more than an hour of the around the clock business at this main office. Scouting of the entrances and exits had only taken a few trips downtown and the one-way streets made this an easy target.

Having gathered barricade materials such as an old stove, refrigerator and old junk Ford Pinto, some newly purchased chains and locks along with a trusty standby, a 55-gallon barrel, we were ready. The junk car was to be towed by a fourwheel drive Subaru Brat with the barrel in the back. Our group consisting of people from Mesquite, Fort Worth and Dallas left east Dallas before dawn on September 23, 1983 to carry out the last full-scale action of the Comanche Peak Life Force.

After a quick drive south to Main Street some folks parked and exited their vehicles with chains and locks to secure the south entrance to the DP&L building. While the rest of us made our way around the corner to Browder Street where we quickly dropped off the stove and refrigerator. Just as quickly these were chained together and then locked to doors of the building. Going completely unnoticed we rounded the corner to Commerce Street and the main entrance doors just as the Brat towing the Pinto and carrying the 55-gallon barrel adorned with a radiation symbol pulled up and onto the sidewalk. In a moments time we had parked the blockade car directly in front of the doors. Using more chains and locks we had securely closed the offices of Dallas Power and Light. About this time the surprised security guards took notice and called the Dallas Police Department which responded with four squad cars and eight officers.

Three of our non-violent urban guerilla band chained themselves to front doors while two more climbed atop the parapet over the entrance where a banner reading "Rate Payers Force Closure—Must Sell Nuke Plant" was unfurled. After more than an hour the five activists were arrested for obstructing a highway and trespassing, then released on bond later in the day. Those arrested included Mavis Belisle, Jim Schermbeck, Sally Mitchell along with two others. Not wanting a public forum, Dallas Power and Light had the charges dropped. Having helped in the barricades around the building, Kent and I chose the Coyote method of "hit and run" rather than getting arrested. After a short reprieve we were to start the guerilla art campaign of the Paint Bucket Brigade.

The freeways around the Metroplex were packed with billboards, some atop two- story buildings with no security and others free standing within reach of energetic non-violent anti-nuke activists. Supplies were gathered, spray paint, extra-long handled rollers, paint pans and buckets of blue or black paint. The billboards atop buildings were accessed with ease and became early targets. The simple message "No Nukes" was painted, making it as easy as just spelling the two words, seven letters in less than an hour.

The message was again in the public eye. Smaller signs

on the highway to Fort Worth were also utilized with ease. Always with a scout on the lookout and escape routes already discussed, the guerrilla art campaign was carried out with success with only one misspelling that we know of.

The largest and most visible target was the huge concrete embankment at the intersection of Central Expressway and L.B.J. Freeway. This took more planning for the canvas (concrete) was dirty and littered with small pieces of everything from metal, hub caps, beer bottles and the ever-present cigarette butts. That problem was remedied by taking brooms and sweeping the area clean as can be. The next week during a Monday Night Football game the actual art festival took place. NO NUKES. Seven letters, two simple words was the message.

The construction of the Comanche Peak Steam Electric Nuclear Station continued and went online in the spring 0f 1990. The original cost estimate was $779 million, the final cost was over $9 billion. Waste is being stored onsite like most all nuclear power plants in the United States. There is no real long-term plan for how to deal with this highly radioactive waste which will burst into a toxic emitting fire when exposed to air, only ideas, such as burying it for millennia or using it in small munitions for the military war machine. There are no clear plans for decommissioning the nukes, which will no doubt be paid for by the people of the United States, costing more than money in resources. Those of us in the fight against nuclear power and other corporate industries fueled by greed, face the future wondering if we did enough to help the planet? In the end all they are doing

Somervell County jurors are addressed by defense lawyer Lewis Pitts at November trial.

Comanche Peak protesters take their case to the people

By Wendy Watriss

Glen Rose

For the past six months, the citizens of this small North Texas town have been witnessing a rather extraordinary kind of grassroots political protest—a test of Tocqueville's dictum that an informed citizenry is a prerequisite for a functioning democracy. The purpose of the protest is public education. The issue is the people's right to know about the hazards posed by a nuclear power plant. The forum is the courtroom in Somervell County, Texas.

Last June and again this November, the antinuclear movement in Texas made a radical shift. Abandoning the cautious approach of most of the state's antinuclear organizations, a group of people under the auspices of the Dallas-based Comanche Peak Life Force climbed the fence at Texas Utilities' Comanche Peak nuclear plant in Somervell County and were arrested for trespassing. These "occupations" were the first instances of civil disobedience directed against nuclear energy in Texas.

More important than the occupations, however, has been the series of trials which have followed. The trials have attracted scientists, lawyers, and grassroots political organizers from all over the country. They are transforming the small county courtroom in Glen Rose into a focal point for debate on nuclear power—raising questions which are still too rarely heard by the general public.

How did this happen?

Six miles north of Glen Rose, the state's first nuclear power plant is being built. The $1.7 billion project, Comanche Peak Steam Electric Generating Plant, belongs to Texas Utilities, Inc., and is due to begin operation in 1981. If the second of two 1,150-megawatt units goes on line as scheduled in 1983, Comanche Peak will be one of the largest plants in the country—only slightly smaller than the South Texas Nuclear Project at Matagorda Bay. Although some of its power has been sold to Brazos Electric Cooperative and the Texas Municipal Power Agency (*Obs.*, Aug. 11, 1978), most of its electricity is destined for the more than four million people served by Texas Utilities, particularly those in the Dallas-Fort Worth area. By 1990, Comanche Peak is expected to provide power for 15 percent of the total Texas Utilities system, covering a third of the state.

Since 1974, when building began, Comanche Peak has been plagued by the cost overruns and construction problems endemic to all new nuclear plants. But, until recently, it escaped the intense public scrutiny and negative publicity that have helped slow nuclear development in states like Oregon, Oklahoma, New York, and New Hampshire.

The lack of attention is not surprising. The decisions which led to building the plant and locating it near Glen Rose were made by Texas Utilities in the late 1960s, long before most people in Glen Rose, or even Dallas and Fort Worth, were aware of them.

Only 45 miles south of Dallas-Fort Worth, Glen Rose is still a quiet place in a somewhat rural county where retired

is boiling water, making steam for turning turbines and creating deadly waste for future generations to deal with. NO NUKES!!!

TURN OFF THE NUKES
TURN ON THE SUN

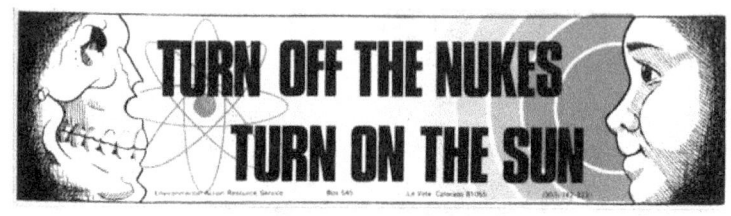

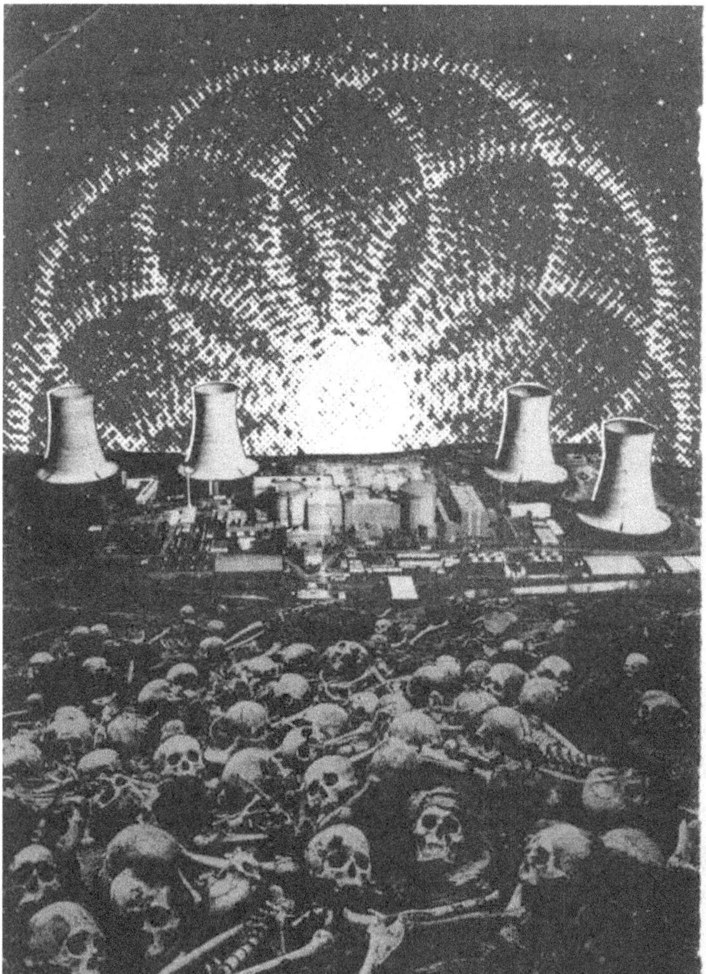

RADIATION ALERT

They're bringing radioactive fuel to Comanche Peak

Beginning in early May, and continuing through August, Texas Utilities will be bringing the enriched uranium fuel to the site of the Comanche Peak nuclear power plant near Glen Rose. It is expected to come by truck from the Westinghouse fabrication facility in Columbia, S.C. About 20 trucks, each carrying six lavendar cannisters of the nuclear fuel, will arrive over a period of several weeks.

Join your voice with ours in protesting this violation of our health and environment. Join us

May 1, at a planning meeting at 6 p.m. at 2710 Woodmere;

May 3, at a showing of the film, "Medical Implications of Nuclear Energy," featuring Dr. Helen Caldicott, at 8 p.m. at First Unitarian Church, Preston at Normandy, Dallas, sponsored by the Armadillo Coalition of Texas.

For information on other activities, contact **Comanche Peak Life Force**, 2710 Woodmere, Dallas, Texas 75233, 214-337-5885.

Early June 2019, 40 years to the week

With a little planning and social media contacts, Jim Schermbeck put together a reunion in Glen Rose for the first weekend of June 2019. Seven of the original forty-eight arrested protesters were able to make it with several more sending their well wishes. Having arrived on Thursday the day before the planned reunion, I rode up to the entrance of Comanche Peak. I also cruised some of the side roads which we had hiked as trails years earlier. Worn out trailers and thickets of mesquite trees were the understory with the ominous twin domes looming in the background. I drove out to Dinosaur State Park for some fly fishing before heading back to the motel.

We gathered at a motel just north of the Paluxy River. After greetings we settled in for a few cold beers and some smoke. Along with the CPLF, Jon Whitsells' daughter and Rick Baraff, a photojournalist from Dallas, rounded out our merry band. Rick was interested in our stories and the trial of the first group of protestors, so it was fun watching him fish us for information.

I shared digital photos taken back in 1979 and 1980, which everyone enjoyed and the catching up with old friends made for a good time. Saturday, early in the afternoon, we piled into a van Jim had rented for us and off we went touring the places we remembered. The Somerville County Courthouse was the first stop. It remained the same, but the town square was now cluttered with reminders of who was the largest contributor to the tax base of the area. A tiny log crib previously located in the Hopewell community of Somerville County served as the local Post Office in the early 1900s. It was relocated before it was flooded in the making of Squaw Creek Lake, the coolant pond of Comanche Peak now part of the town square complete with a pretty flower garden. Also, the Somerville County Museum, which houses the dinosaur tracks in limestone found during construction of the nuclear plant. We then rode a couple of blocks south to the old staging area for the two large occupations in 1979. Surprisingly, the yellow trailer was still there along with the restored ranch house. The current owner of the property was okay with us taking a quick walk around.

Then we drove up to the entrance of the Comanche Peak Nuclear Station, where I quickly explained my idea for one more action and the group was all on board. Having Rick take photos while we poised with an original banner/flag of the CPLF covering the welcome sign, the return of the CPLF 7 was complete. After a nice meal provided by Jim at a local eatery, we returned to the motel for more sharing of memories and merriment. The next day after sharing contact information we all went back to the future.

There's a NUKE in your backyard!

Wake up, Dallas-Fort Worth,

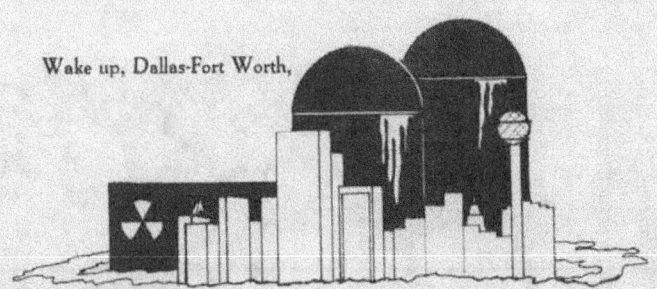

There is a very large and very dangerous nuclear power plant being built near your home. It is called Comanche Peak, and it sits 35 miles southwest of Fort Worth, 60 miles from Dallas, just outside Glen Rose.

Why be concerned?

Comanche Peak will actually be two nuclear reactors, each bigger than anything operating in the country right now. The plant will produce 200 pounds of high level waste each day and will store up to 18 years of the stuff at the site, making it the largest nuclear waste dump in the Southwest. Every day the plant operates it will produce the equivalent of 2000 times the radiation released by the atom bomb dropped on Hiroshima. Some of this radiation will be purposely released into the environment; some of it will escape by accident. In other areas near nuclear power plants cancer, leukemia and numerous other diseases have risen dramatically because of such releases of "low level radiation."

Comanche Peak will only provide Dallas-Fort Worth with 15% of its energy needs at a time when the utilities in the area are vastly overbuilt in electric generating capacity. Comanche Peak has risen in cost from an original estimate of $777 million to $2.3 billion, and the end is not in sight. Ratepayers are paying for construction of the plant even though it is not yet producing electricity, through a process called CWIP.

Is there an alternative?

We think there is. We believe that the non-nuclear majority of Comanche Peak's equipment can be used to operate a biomass steam electric plant. This process is called "conversion." By utilizing local resources we can avoid the hazards of nuclear power while giving a boost to safer and cheaper solar produced energy. A biomass Comanche Peak would also mean more jobs than a nuclear power plant will provide.

NO NUKES here and now

So what can you do? Join those of us who've decided to expose Comanche Peak for what it is -- a big white elephant that is a threat to our health and to our pocketbooks. The Comanche Peak Life Force is involved in a continuing campaign to educate and demonstrate against the plant, and we need all the help we can get. If you've been sitting on the fence, now is the time to get to work. The plant is due on line in 1982. There's no time to waste if we want a nuclear-free future for ourselves and for our children.

Comanche Peak Life Force

Dallas: 824-4565, 337-5883   Austin: 478-7481   Glen Rose: 897-4110

NUCLEAR POWER PLANT: A FANCY WAY TO BOIL WATER: In the reactor core the fuel rods go through the fission process. The atoms of uranium are split, and heat is produced. The heat raises the temperature of water to make steam, the steam drives a turbine and the mechanical energy from the moving turbine blades is converted into electrical energy through a generator and sent out of the plant over power lines. (diagram: cutaway reactor)

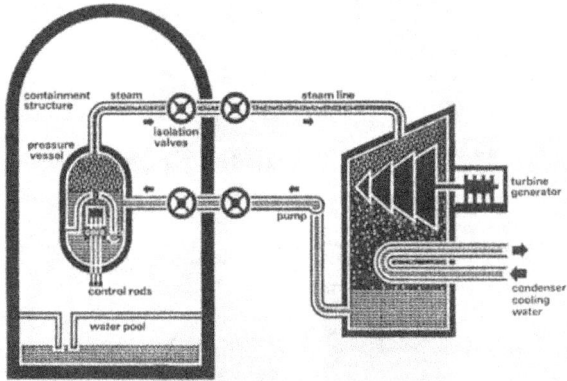

Cutaway of Nuclear Reactor

There are many risks and hazards at the nuclear plant:

1. The nuclear reactor routinely releases vapors (low-level radiation) into the air which have radioactive poisons in them. The health of the people living near nuclear power plants has grown worse.⁴

2. Workers are often exposed to various amounts of radioactivity in operating the plants.

3. Workers' clothing, tools, machinery and work areas of the plant can become contaminated with radioactivity.

4. Since water is used to cool the very hot fuel rods, there must be a constant flushing through the cooling system of the plant. Some radioactive water is accidentally discharged and sent back into the rivers, oceans and lakes that support and feed life (diagram)

5. There is the possibility that the fuel rods will become too hot if something goes wrong with the cooling system or if something else major fails to work in the plant. If this happens the fuel rods will melt to the bottom of the reactor vessel, through the concrete floor of the plant and out into the ground. This is called a **meltdown** and has the potential for releasing disastrous amounts of radioactive poisons. A government study published in 1957 showed that a meltdown could kill as many as 3,400, injure 43,000, cause $7 billion worth of damage and contaminate an area the size of the state of Pennsylvania.⁴

The nuclear fuel cycle does not end at the nuclear power plant. The rest of the cycle is called the Back End.

PLANT LIFE AND DECOMMISSIONING: Nuclear reactors work for only about 30 years. After this time they must be **decommissioned.** Decommissioning means disposing of the plant itself which by then is radioactive and must be dismantled, buried, or in some way kept from living things.

WASTES: The contaminated clothing, tools, machinery, etc. are called **low level wastes.** The nuclear industry has been storing most low level wastes in shallow trenches in a number of places throughout the US. These are only temporary storage places and there have been many occurrences of radioactivity moving away from the storage sites and into the ground and water.⁷

HIGH LEVEL WASTES: In the fission process new elements are made. These include strontium 90, cesium 137, plutonium 239, iodine 131, and many others. They are all radioactive, very hot and poisonous. They are man-made elements that must be kept cool and

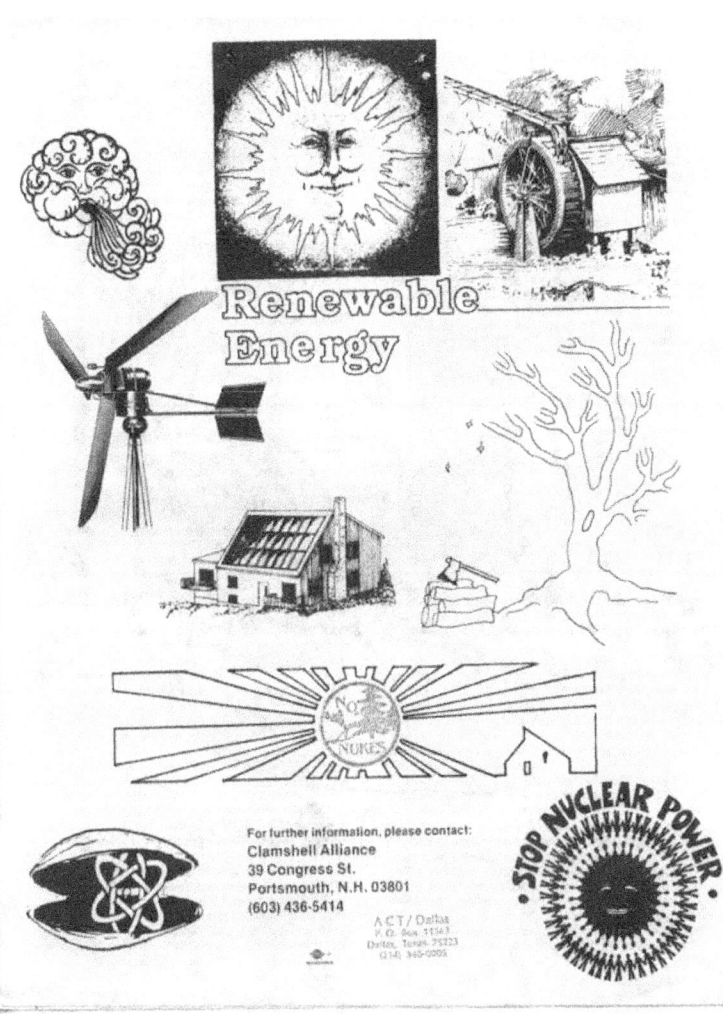

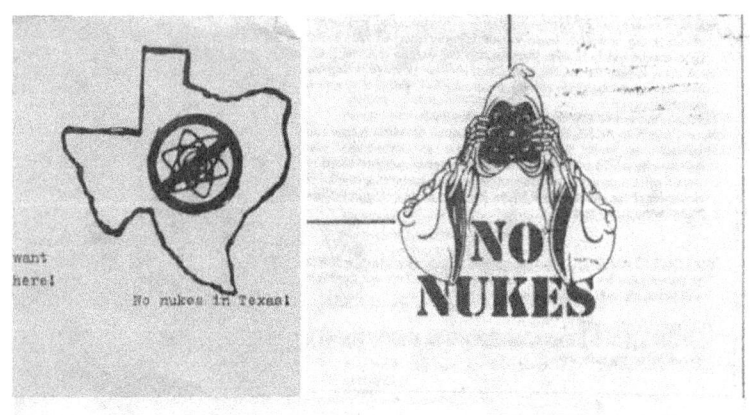

Epilogue

The original Comanche Peak Life Force lasted through the protest of the Republican National Convention in August of 1984. The members of the CPLF became involved in other environmental and social justice issues and some even sought political office. I continued my work as an arborist in Dallas until moving back to Mississippi in 1987. I worked for a family owned landscape company until being hired work as the assistant golf course superintendent at Colonial Country Club in Jackson, Mississippi in 1989. I studied to become a Master Gardener, through training provided by Mississippi State Extension Service, I was able to encourage the use of native plants with heirloom roses and bulbs into the landscape of 160 acres of the Colonial Country Club until leaving in 2012. The people in the native plant community in the southeastern United States helped reinforce my passion as a tree hugger and overall Greenie. A side note: from the country club property, I was able to recuse dozens of the old roses and bulbs with permission of the owner after the property was sold, many more were liberated without permission.

My resolve on issues of pollution led me to become involved in river cleanups and continuing to speak out against the blatant disregard of the environment by individuals and corporations. While encouraging the preservation and use of native plants, less reliance on chemicals in gardening and the benefits of composting. Along with years of doing plant rescues (mostly with permission) and guerilla gardening, I began realizing you can catch more flies with honey than vinegar, I try to share my knowledge of gardening and caring for a greener world, one garden at a time. Continuing as an estate gardener and owner of Lycoris Rose, a southern heirloom bulb farm, my goal is to be a good steward of the Earth.

May 20, 2020
Jerry Palmer

Profile and/or Comments from Contributors

Cynthia Rutledge: When I heard about the nuclear power plant planned for Glen Rose, it only seemed right to protest such an unsafe, unnecessary, and wasteful project. Most people in north Texas were completely unaware that a nuclear plant would be in our area. As construction progressed, we heard stories of corners being cut and unskilled workers making mistakes. This certainly didn't calm fears about safety.

I met a lot of people from all walks of life in the Comanche Peak Life Force, and I remember them as sincere people who saw a wrong and who were committed to trying to make it right. Peaceful civil disobedience was chosen as the method to protest and I think it was quite successful. No, we failed in shutting the plant down for good. But, thanks to publicity generated for several years, including the largest act of civil disobedience ever seen in Glen Rose, Texas people were made aware of the plant, and the controversies surrounding the concept of nuclear power in general.

Jim Schermbeck: Texas Legacy Project.... a long-time environmental community organizer in DFW. He opened the Dallas office of the national Toxics Campaign in 1989, and then moved to Downwinders at Risk in 1994, where he continues the good fight.

Mavis Belisle: Texas Legacy Project.... continues as a peace and justice activist and organizer while on the board of directors at the Dallas Peace Center.

Mavis Belisle: written July 22, 2020

For many of us, opposition to the Comanche Peak nuclear plant began with an organization called the Armadillo Coalition.

We began meeting at UT Arlington, then moved to locations in Dallas and Fort Worth. We did all the expected organizing things—study groups, press conferences, worked with existing groups on the licensing intervention etc. There was press interest, but the utilities yarned. Occasionally we debated but they were condescending to the point of rudeness. And then the landscape changed.

A group in New Hampshire called the Clamshell Alliance, opposing the Seabrook nuclear power plant, began to engage in large-scale civil disobedience. Hundreds were arrested. Through civil disobedience had been done by other groups around the country, it was not on that scale or with their spirit. Like dry grass that caught fire, groups across the country upped civil disobedience in their actions. In the Armadillo Coalition, there were voices pro and con as we discussed civil disobedience, and we decided to form a separate group rather than split the coalition. The new group became the Comanche Peak Life Force.

We began looking for nonviolence training and recruited two trainers from Oklahoma. That were opposing the Black Fox nuclear plant and had carried out civil disobedience actions before.

We sent out announcements thru the local media and then gathered at Lee Park in Dallas, hoping trainees would show up. They did.

We met Sundays at Lee Park for several months and began meeting in affinity groups to get to know each other and plan an action. We also went door to door in Glen Rose, explaining what we were doing along with information about the nuclear plant and its dangers. Doing this canvassing work, we met a local landowner who would let us camp on his land on the Paluxy River.

Jim Schermbeck and I also went to an antinuclear event near Gallup in New Mexico on Dine (Navajo) land. The event included Dine, Hispanic and white groups, all camping separately. A group of Japanese Buddhist nuns drummed continuously on a slope nearby. Finally, on the last day, the Dine invited all of us to join them in a morning blessing ceremony, casting a new spirituality over all our work.

While there, we recruited Lewis Pitts, our lawyer. He joined us in Dallas soon after to find a Texas attorney to join him, and he found Tom Mills. Tom had not defended civil disobedience before, but was interested and willing, and our legal team was formed.

Holly Whitson: continued to advocate for environmental protection and indigenous land and water rights issues as a law student and an attorney. Today, she is an attorney in Denver, Colorado fighting mass incarceration and the death penalty.

Lewis Pitts: after forty years of fighting the good fight, accumulating many awards and recognitions of his work on children's rights, economic and social justice, Lewis was so troubled by what he perceived to be the common practice of attorneys and law firms to put making money above goals of seeking justice that he pushed the North Carolina Bar to establish a procedure for resigning from the profession. As of April,2014 he is a practicing nonlawyer focusing on public interest.

Reflections on Comanche Peak Resistance in Texas from Lewis Pitts… written August 2020

I certainly have fond, if fuzzy after all these years, memories of the fine folks who made up the Comanche Peak Life Force. They fought the construction of that plant with all their heart, soul, and creative powers. I was certainly fortunate to be invited to offer some legal assistance for planning and defending their civil disobedience action in, the Summer of 1979.

True to the reputation of Texas, many strong, independent, justice loving women and men

> Hell no
> we won't glow
> we won't glow
> for LILCO —
>
> Hey y'all —
> Quite a weekend for an action. Had a great time. Wish 47,000 more folks had come. Truly tho it was a good time. Hope your weekend was as good — rain + all! CPLF made lots of new friends and gained lots of respect as news of the spirit filtered across the staging area and blockade and jail and ferry. Cynthia can fill you in on all the details — let's just say the solidarity helped and is returned. Would've been more fun in Texas, but it was ok for the Northeast, huh? We'll show 'em next time!
> No Nukes!
> Peace —
> Holly

organized several different forms of non-violent civil disobedience and trespassing onto the site of the Comanche Peak plant. While I don't recall nearly all of those fine people, several folks like Mavis Belisle, Jerry Palmer, Jim Schermbeck stand out as key leaders. Also, Dallas criminal defense attorney Tom Mills volunteered to defend them for no fee. His invitation to me and motion to the court for me to participate with him is what allowed me, who was not admitted to the Texas "Bar" to be one of the lawyers.

As I recall, the first trespass action was well planned and even coordinated with the Comanche Peak officials and local law enforcement. That way the risk of law enforcement violence and ridiculously serious criminal charges were minimized. This fact *made it easier for more people to join the "action" either to get arrested or be present to be in support of the very important anti-nuclear cause and to assist those getting arrested with bail and other support efforts if they remained in jail. Subsequent actions of civil disobedience that came the next months were more rambunctious and included some folks sneaking onto Comanche Peak property, hiding, and forcing law enforcement to try and capture them. Creative stuff that surely makes Populist Texans like John Henry Faulk, Molly Ivins, Jim Hightower, and maybe even former Texas Governor Ann Richards, immensely proud.*

News accounts can provide exact details but the "defense" in the first set of arrests was legally called "duress and necessity." Simply put, that meant those arrested were non-violent and acted from their sincere belief that the building and operating of nuclear power plants created a serious danger and harm to the people, animals, plants, and the land in a large area nearby. Therefore, those arrested acted out of necessity and under duress and were compelled to take action to draw attention to end the threat of harm and even death. Another way to look at this defense is to weigh and select the lesser harm being done: which is more dangerous or wrong, building the radioactive power plant that emits dangerous radiation even under normal conditions OR peacefully climbing over the fence to the nuclear property and trespassing to draw attention to the issue? Another example is if your neighbor's backyard is on fire and you break into her/his garage with minimal force to grab a shovel to put out the brush fire, is that a criminal offense of breaking and entering? Or were you acting due to necessity? Your intent in doing the action is important in whether you should be deemed culpable or liable for those actions.

I wish there were a transcript from the trial of the powerful testimony given by the "demonstrators" about their deep knowledge about the radiation dangers and their moral and ethical beliefs giving rise to their acts of civil disobedience. Hopefully, they can provide such important historical information.

Tom Mills, defense attorney:

I started practicing criminal defense and Constitutional law in Texas in 1972. During summers while in University of Texas law school I had worked at the Washington DC Public Defender Office, so I had some slight knowledge of "what to do" in criminal court. My primary clients were SMU students accused of marijuana possession. The smallest, tiniest amount of marijuana carried up to a life sentence in Texas until 1974. So, no one wanted to plead guilty to a felony- even probation- and the police frequently arrested everyone in an apartment room if they found a roach in an ashtray even though they couldn't prove whose marijuana it was. So, I had numerous hearings and trials. The cases I defended were in State criminal courts, which I enjoyed, but I also wanted to learn to try cases in federal court.

A lawyer friend asked me to go to a (small) monthly Dallas ACLU meeting at Hank Albach's house, and I was interested in some of their potential civil rights litigation. Hank, his wife, his son John and his wife, Judy Time, Fred Time were the most active people that I knew in the Dallas ACLU. I was the only active trial lawyer in the group. The ACLU was then and is now controversial, especially in Dallas, which was more conservative then than it is now, and I knew "being in the ACLU" would not be even dreamed of by many Dallas people, but just being a criminal defense lawyer was controversial enough with some people, and participating in the litigation, or solely doing the litigation would allow me to learn federal litigation. My trial lawyer on-the-job-training was parallel to young lawyers my age who were working at a DA's Office, then often moving to the US Attorney's Office.

When people called the Dallas ACLU office, the calls would be screened and some of the people who left messages about possible civil rights violations were given my name to talk to. My experience was fantastic because I got to try to help people and try cases in front of Judges Sarah T. Hughes, (she had sworn me in as a lawyer) Pat Higgenbotham, Jerry Buchmeyer, William Wayne Justice, and other excellent and interesting Judges.

Probably, from some connection I made through this group, I got a call in 1978 or 1979 about representing one or more protesters who had been arrested at the Comanche Peak Nuclear Power Plant in Glen Rose, Somervell County, Texas. I believe that they had chained themselves to a gate entering the property. They would be or had been charged with trespassing.

I met some of the group, including some nuns from Dallas or the Dallas area. Glen Rose, where the courthouse was, was 75 miles southwest of Dallas. I of course volunteered to help represent one or more of them. I became friends with Sister Patricia, one of the defendants, but I don't remember all the details about how many people were going to trial in what turned out to be the first trial or how many I represented at that trial. Lawyer from Lewis Pitts, from South Carolina, was really lead counsel, and I loved his personality and easy way of dealing with people. He had experience and skills that I did not have in organizing groups or advising groups about educating the public on important issues. Like the danger of even low-level radiation. We knew the jury would be from the town and the area and that they were largely farmers and ranchers.

Ken Nelson aka Albert Most:

Author of *Bufo Alvarius: The Psychedelic Toad of the Sonoran Desert* published by Venom Press in 1984. He worked at the Comanche Peak nuke providing valuable information during the planning stages of our guerilla actions. He also brewed the mead and cooked up the smoke bomb for the July,1980 action. He passed in the summer of 2019, leaving a legacy of merry-making, modern alchemy and a continuous quest for knowledge.

LEFT: Road Gang Blockade. March 28, 1980
RIGHT: Author Crossing Fence. June 10, 1979

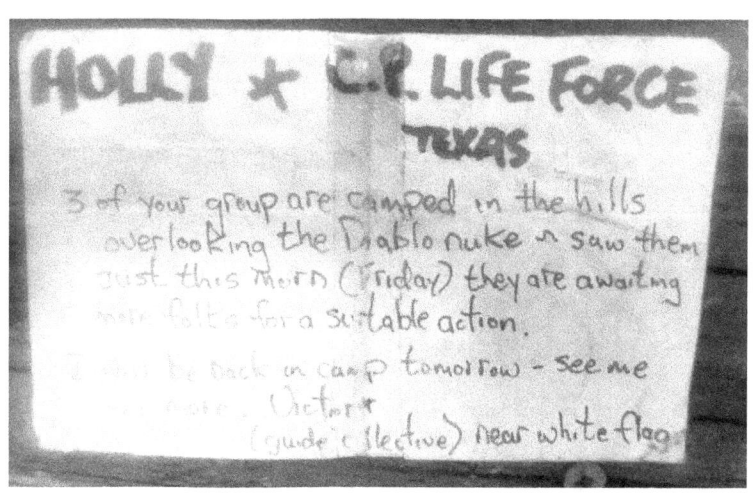

Note from bulletin board.
Diablo Canyon, September 1981

Song written during July 1980 occupation

June the tenth of '79' forty-eight people crossed the line. Used some ladders and we crossed the fence. We took it to trial and got to walk away, only to be tried another day. No Nukes!! No Nukes!! around here.

November 25, 103 folks used those ladders and jumped the fence and said "look, judge its self- defense." No Nukes!! No Nukes around here.

On the morning of March 28th, the Road Gang was formed, and we hit the gate. Used some chains and a washing machine, all the workers wondered 'what does this mean?' No Nukes!! No Nukes around here.

July the 4th the woods came alive, choppers started swarming like bees in a hive. Sitting in my hammock writing this song, wishing all you people had come along, stand up now, don't hesitate, we got to stop Comanche before it's too late No Nukes!! No Nukes!! No Nukes around here.

Methane gas, wind and bright sunshine will give us electricity all the time. No Nukes!! No Nukes!! around here.

Written by Kent Wilson & Jerry Palmer, July 1980

www.ingramcontent.com/pod-product-compliance
Lightning Source LLC
Chambersburg PA
CBHW050314120526
44592CB00014B/1910